BARRON'S

COMMON CORE SUCCESS
LEARN, REVIEW, APPLY

GRADE 2 ENGLISH LANGUAGE ARTS

what's your STORY

Jodi DeSantis-Helming

Consulting Editor

All inquiries should be addressed to:
Barron's Educational Series, Inc.
250 Wireless Boulevard
Hauppauge, NY 11788
www.barronseduc.com

ISBN 978-1-4380-0671-0

Library of Congress Control Number: 2014957249

Date of Manufacture: June 2015
Manufactured by: C&C Offset Printing Co., Ltd, Shenzhen, China

Printed in China

9 8 7 6 5 4 3 2 1

As of August 2013, forty-six states and the District of Columbia had adopted the Common Core State Standards (CCSS) for English Language Arts (ELA) literacy and mathematics. These standards are geared toward preparing students for college, careers, and competition in the global economy. The adoption of the CCSS represents the first time that schools across the nation have had a common set of expectations for what students should know and be able to do. As with any new program, there are growing pains associated with implementation. Teachers are busy adapting classroom materials to meet the standards, and many parents are confused about what the standards mean for their children. As such, it is a prime opportunity for the creation of a workbook series that provides a clear-cut explanation of the standards coupled with effective lessons and activities tied to those standards.

The foundation of Barron's English Language Arts (ELA) literacy workbook for the second grade is based on sound educational practices coupled with parent-friendly explanations of the standards and interesting activities for students that meet those standards. While many other workbook series on the market today offer students practice with individual skills outlined in the CCSS, none seem to do so in a cohesive manner. Our goal was to create an exciting series that mirrors the way teachers actually teach in the classroom. Rather than random workbook pages that present each of the CCSS skills in isolation, our series presents the skills in interesting units of related materials that reinforce each of the standards in a meaningful way. We have included Stop and Think (Review/Understand/Discover) sections to assist parents/tutors and students in applying those skills at a higher level. The standards being addressed in each unit are clearly labeled and explained throughout so that parents/tutors have a better grasp of the purpose behind each activity. Additionally, second graders will be familiar and comfortable with the manner of presentation and learning as this is what they should be accustomed to in their everyday school experiences. These factors will not only assist students in mastering the skills of the standards for second grade, but will also provide an opportunity for parents to play a larger role in their children's overall education. Finally, the pedagogical stance of these workbooks will allow Barron's publishing to reach a wider audience. It is our view that it is not only parents and their children who will be able to use these books, but also tutors and teachers!

Lisa Wilson, M.Ed
Amy Owens, NBCT El. Ed

Common Core Standards for English Language Arts

The following explanation of educational goals is based on the Common Core English Language Arts standards that your child will learn in the second grade. A comprehensive list of the Common Core State Standards can be viewed at the following website: *www.corestandards.org*.

Understanding Standard Labels:

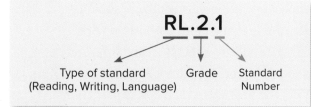

RL.2.1

Type of standard
(Reading, Writing, Language)   Grade   Standard Number

Reading: Foundational Skills (RF)

Phonics and Word Recognition

(Standards RF.2.3.a, RF.2.3.b, RF.2.3.c, RF.2.3.d, RF.2.3.e, and RF.2.3.f)

Your child will do/learn the following:

- Distinguish between long and short vowels when reading one-syllable words.
- Know spelling-sound correspondence for additional common vowels.
- Decode two-syllable words with long vowels.
- Decode words with common prefixes and suffixes.
- Identify words with inconsistent but common spelling-sound correspondences.
- Recognize and read grade-appropriate irregularly spelled words.

Fluency

(Standards RF.2.4.a, RF.2.4.b, and RF.2.4.c)

Your child will do/learn the following:

- Read on-level text with purpose and understanding.
- Read on-level text orally with accuracy, appropriate rate, and expression.
- Use context to confirm or self-correct word recognition and understanding, rereading as necessary.

Reading Standards

(RI: Reading Informational Texts, RL: Reading Literature)

Key Ideas and Details

(Standards RI.2.1, RI.2.2, RI.2.3, RL.2.1, RL.2.2, and RL.2.3)

Your child will do/learn the following:

- Ask and answer questions such as who, what, where, when, why, and how to show understanding of key details in informational texts.
- Identify the main topic of multiparagraph texts or from a specific paragraph in informational texts.

- Describe the connection between historical events in informational texts.
- Describe the connection between scientific ideas or concepts, or steps in a procedure in informational texts.
- Ask and answer questions such as who, what, where, when, why, and how to show understanding of key details in literary texts.
- Retell stories, including fables and folktales, in literary texts.
- Determine the central message, lesson, or moral in literary texts.
- Describe how characters respond to events and challenges in literary texts.

Craft and Structure
(Standards RI.2.4, RI.2.5, RI.2.6, RL.2.4, RL.2.5, and RL.2.6)

Your child will do/learn the following:

- Determine the meaning of words and phrases in informational texts.
- Know and use text features (e.g., captions, bold print, subheadings, glossaries, indexes, etc.) to locate key facts or information within informational texts.
- Identify the main purpose of an informational text.
- Answer, explain, or describe the main purpose of an informational text.
- Describe how words and phrases give rhythm and meaning to stories, poems, or songs in literary texts.
- Describe the structure of a story using beginning, middle, and end in literary texts.
- Acknowledge differences in points of view of characters by speaking in different voices for each character in literary texts.

Integration of Knowledge and Ideas
(Standards RI.2.7, RI.2.8, RI.2.9, RL.2.7, and RL.2.9)

Your child will do/learn the following:

- Explain how images contribute to and clarify an informational text.
- Describe how reasons support specific points the author makes in an informational text.
- Compare and contrast the most important points in two texts on the same topic in informational texts.

- Use illustrations and words to demonstrate understanding of the characters, setting, and plot of a literary text.
- Compare and contrast two or more versions of the same story by different authors or cultures.

Writing Standards (W)

Text Types and Purposes
(Standards W.2.1, W.2.2, and W.2.3)

Your child will do/learn the following:

- Write opinion pieces that include introducing the topic, stating an opinion, supplying reasons that support the opinion, using linking words to connect opinion and reasons, and providing a concluding statement or section.
- Write informative/explanatory texts in which they introduce a topic, use facts and definitions to develop points, and provide a concluding statement or section.
- Write narratives where they recount a well-elaborated event or short sequence of events; include details to describe actions, thoughts, and feelings; use temporal words to signal event order; and provide a sense of closure.

Production and Distribution of Writing
(Standards W.2.5 and W.2.6)

With the help of an adult or peer, your child will do/learn the following:

- Focus on a topic and strengthen writing as needed by revising and editing.
- Use a variety of digital tools to produce and publish writing.

Research to Build and Present Knowledge
(Standards W.2.7 and W.2.8)

Your child will do/learn the following:

- Participate in a shared research and writing project (e.g., read a number of books on a single topic to produce a report).
- Recall information from experiences or gather information from provided sources to answer a question.

Language Standards (L)

Conventions of Standard English
(Standards L.2.1.a, L.2.1.b, L.2.1.c, L.2.1.d, L.2.1.e, L.2.1.f, L.2.2.a, L.2.2.b, L.2.2.c, L.2.2.d, and L.2.2.e)

Your child will do/learn the following:

- Use collective nouns.
- Form and use irregular plural nouns.
- Use reflexive pronouns (myself, ourselves).
- Form and use past tense irregular verbs.
- Use adjectives and adverbs, and choose between them depending on what is to be modified.
- Produce, expand, and rearrange complete simple and compound sentences.
- Capitalize proper nouns (holidays, product names, and geographic names).
- Use commas in greetings and closings of letters.
- Use an apostrophe to form contractions and possessives.
- Generalize learned spelling patterns when writing words
- Consult reference materials, including dictionaries, as needed to check and correct spelling.

Knowledge of Language
(Standard L.2.3.a)

Your child will do/learn the following:

- Compare formal and informal uses of English.

Vocabulary Acquisition and Use
(Standards L.2.4.a, L.2.4.b, L.2.4.c, L.2.4.d, L.2.4.e, L.2.5.a L.2.5.b, and L.2.6)

Your child will do/learn the following:

- Use sentence context as a clue to determine the meaning of a word or phrase.
- Determine the meaning of a new word formed when a known prefix is added to a known word.
- Use a known root word as a clue to the meaning of an unknown word with the same root.
- Use knowledge of the meaning of individual words to predict the meaning of compound words.
- Use glossaries and beginning dictionaries to determine and clarify the meaning of words and phrases.
- Identify real-life connections between words and their use.
- Distinguish shades of meaning among closely related verbs (e.g., toss, throw, hurl) and closely related adjectives (e.g., thin, slender, skinny, scrawny).
- Use words and phrases acquired through conversations, reading and being read to, and responding to texts, including using adjectives and adverbs to describe.

Contents

Contents

Reading:
Foundational Skills

Recognizing Phonics and Words

In this first section, you will review skills that form the very foundation of your reading abilities. For this reason, they are called foundational skills. The Common Core State Standards have identified this set of skills as being important to master in order to become a fluent and effective reader. Phonics and fluency are at the center of reading and learning. For the fluency section, be sure an adult is available to keep time as you read aloud.

We hope you enjoy reviewing these important skills as you progress through your Common Core journey to excellence.

Happy reading!

When reading, how do you pronounce an unknown word? This can be very challenging, especially if it is a hard word. In this first section, you will review strategies in phonics. These tools will help you to understand familiar words quickly and figure out words that you have not seen before.

This first section will provide a strong foundation for developing reading fluency. Let's begin!

SHORT AND LONG VOWEL SOUNDS

Short vowel sounds are very quick to say. There are only five of them:

> a as in **c<u>a</u>t**
> e as in **p<u>e</u>t**
> i as in **f<u>i</u>t**
> o as in **p<u>o</u>t**
> u as in **c<u>u</u>t**

When you say a **long vowel** sound, you stretch out the sound. Like short vowel sounds, there are only five long vowel sounds:

> a as in **h<u>a</u>te**
> e as in **<u>e</u>ve**
> i as in **b<u>i</u>te**
> o as in **n<u>o</u>**
> u as in **c<u>u</u>te**

As you can see, many one-syllable words with long vowel sounds often end in a silent "e."

Activity 1

Circle the correct answer for each question.

1. Which word uses a **short vowel** sound?
   A. drip
   B. cage
   C. base

2. Which word uses a **long vowel** sound?
   A. bite
   B. bid
   C. bed

Activity 2

Answer each question below.

1. Circle the word that has the same short vowel sound as **bit**.

Mei sat on top of the cliff and saw the bright sunshine sparkle on the ocean waves.

2. Circle the word that has the same short vowel sound as **fed**.

Marcy's pet dog, Hugo, wagged his fluffy tail after she gave him a tasty treat.

3. Circle the word that has the same short vowel sound as **hot**.

Juan's mom told him to stop at home and get a hat.

4. Circle the word that has the same short vowel sound as **cut**.

Elijah's dad told him to rub soap into his coat to get a stain out.

Activity 3

Circle the words that have long vowel sounds in them.

Matt and his dad saw a white bird in a tree. His dad said Matt should name the bird, so Matt called it "Steve."

Standard RF.2.3.b

VOWEL TEAMS

Vowel teams are the superheroes of words. They are two letters that work together to make a word sound a certain way. The letters used in vowel teams are **a**, **e**, **i**, **o**, **u**, **w**, and **y**.

For many of these teams, only the first letter is heard when spoken.

For example, **ai** sounds like a long a in the word **aim**. This is also true for the vowel team **ay** (**stay**).

The chart shows other vowel teams.

Vowel Team	Sound	Example Word	Example Sentence
ea	long e	lead	Martin will <u>lead</u> the group today.
ee	long e	seed	Rosario planted <u>seeds</u> in her garden.
ew	long u	flew	The bird <u>flew</u> away when it heard a noise.
oa	long o	boat	Tyrell sailed a <u>boat</u> across the sea.
oo	long u	tool	Sonya built a table using special <u>tools</u>.
ue	long u	true	Max's story about seeing a moose was <u>true</u>.

Activity 1

Match the vowel team sound with the correct word.

1. Long a   a. toad

2. Long e   b. paid

3. Long o   c. sheep

Activity 2

Now, circle the words in the sentences that use vowel teams.

1. Darnell got a new coat for school.

2. Lori grew flowers that were blue.

3. Ernesto wanted to wait by the tree.

4. Jada's dog likes to eat and play.

Activity 3

Fill in the blanks with the correct vowel team for each word. Use the word bank to help you.

1. Jamal used gl __ __ to fix a broken vase.

2. Chen washed her face with s __ __ p and water.

3. Mario could not wait to r __ __ d his new book.

4. Amy learned to swim in a p __ __ l.

word bank

ea

oa

oo

ue

Activity 4

How many words can you make by filling in the blanks with vowel teams? List the words that you can think of on the first line. Try not to form a word that is already in the chart on page 15.

1. h __ __ d

_____

2. f __ __ l

_____

3. h __ __ l

_____

4. b __ __ t

_____

Words with Vowel Teams

Digging Deeper

You probably know many words that use vowel teams. Cut out 14 rectangles from thick paper or thin cardboard. Write one letter on each card. There should be 2 cards each for a, e, i, o, u, w, and y. Decorate the back of each card with bright colors or pictures from magazines.

When you have made your new "deck" of cards, shuffle the deck. Draw two cards. Have you created a vowel team? If so, make a word that uses the vowel team.

Ask a friend to play with you. See how many words you and your friend can make together!

LONG VOWEL SOUNDS IN TWO-SYLLABLE WORDS

Two-syllable words can have just long vowel sounds in them. These words look the way they are spelled.

> For example, another word for **woman** is **female**.
>
> fe + male
>
> For the word **female**, the first syllable **fe** has a long **e** sound. The second syllable, **male**, has a long **a** sound.
>
> Did you notice that the syllable **male** ends with an **e** that is silent? This is because many words or syllables with long vowel sounds end with a silent **e**. Other words with long vowel sounds that also end with a silent **e** are **pine**, **bone**, **same**, and **tune**.

Activity 1

Read each question. Then circle the correct answer.

1. Which day of the week uses a long vowel in both syllables?

    A. Monday   B. Thursday   C. Friday

2. Which word uses a long vowel sound in both syllables?

    A. hayride   B. football   C. doctor

Activity 2

Use the word bank to complete the activity.

1. Paul has soccer practice after school to_____.

2. Kate's mother bakes _____made bread.

3. A honey bee lives in a _____hive.

word bank

bee

fire

day

home

Challenge: Circle the two-syllable words that only use long vowel sounds in the paragraph below.

Pham's grandfather is her hero. Every summer, he invites Pham and all her friends to a baseball game. *Maybe this year my team will win,* she thinks.

PREFIXES AND SUFFIXES

Have you ever put on a special hat or shoes to act like someone different? Prefixes and suffixes work the same way. Prefixes are placed before a root word. Suffixes are placed after a root word. When these word parts are connected to the root word, the meaning of the whole word changes.

> **Example:** I have an unusual pet puppy dog, who barks every morning at 6:00 a.m.
>
> The **prefix** un- means **not** or **opposite of**.
>
> The **root word** usual means something that is common or ordinary. Therefore, the word unusual means something that is <u>not usual</u> or not common.

Activity 1

Answer the questions below.

1. Add **un-** to the word **locked**.   un + locked = unlocked

    What does **unlocked** mean? _____

    _____

2. What does the word **hope** mean?   hope + ful = hopeful

    The suffix **-ful** means **full of**. What happens if you place **-ful** after **hope**?

    What does the word **hopeful** mean? _____

    _____

3. Add **-ful** after the word **care**.   care + ful = careful

    What does the word **careful** mean? _____

    _____

Standard RF.2.3.d

Activity 2

Read the table. Then complete the activity below.

Prefix	Suffix	Meaning	Example	Meaning of Example
re-		again	re + try = retry	to try something again
	-er	person who does something	paint + er	someone who paints
	-est	the most of all	hard + est = hardest	the most hard or difficult
	-less	without	help + less = helpless	without help

Match each word to its meaning.

1. helper   a. to build something again

2. biggest   b. without sleep

3. sleepless   c. a person who helps

4. rebuild   d. the most big

Activity 3

Use the best word from the box below to complete the prefix or suffix word in each sentence.

word bank

play

small

teach

happy

1. The new _____er taught the class her name.

2. Isabella was un_____ because she missed the party.

3. Re_____ that song because I like it so much!

4. Paolo picked the _____est piece of cake for dessert

HOMOPHONES

Have you ever heard a group of people sing the same song? The song sounds the same, but the singers all look different! Homophones work the same way. These words are spelled differently and have different meanings, but they sound the same.

> The words **night** and **knight** are homophones. The word **night** means the time of day when it is dark outside. The word **knight** means a type of soldier from the past. See how these words are used in the same sentence:
>
> The knight rode his horse all night long to deliver a message to the king.
>
> The words **blew** and **blue** are also homophones. **Blew** is the past tense of **blow**. It means to make air move. **Blue** is a color. Read these words in the sentence below:
>
> A strong wind blew from the bright blue sky.

Activity 1

Place the correct word in the blank space for each sentence.

1. _____ right to watch _____ step when walking on an icy sidewalk.

   (your, you're)

2. Tran's uncle stayed at an _____ when he was _____ town.

   (inn, in)

Activity 2

Circle the homophone that best completes each sentence.

1. The soccer players won _____ game.

   A. there

   B. they're

   C. their

2. Shoshana wanted _____ play with her best friend, Tanika.

   A. to

   B. too

   C. two

Activity 3

Circle the words in each sentence that are spelled differently but sound the same.

1. It's time to return the book about boats to its shelf.

2. Ms. Stuart knew her class would welcome the new student.

3. William told his father that the deer was a very dear animal.

4. To smell the scent of a rose does not cost a cent.

Activity 4

Match the words that sound alike.

1. eight   a. pour

2. poor   b. hour

3. our   c. hole

4. whole   d. ate

Activity 5

Use each of these words in a sentence.

1. sail _____

   sale _____

2. meet _____

   meat _____

IRREGULAR WORDS

Why does *do* not rhyme with *so* or *no*? Why is *said* not spelled like *red* or *bed*? That is because these words, along with hundreds of others, are not spelled in a regular way. Because of this, they are called **irregular** words. Although they may seem hard to read and understand at first, we use many of them every day.

Activity 1

Match the words that have the same sound spelled different ways.

1. four   a. true

2. high   b. son

3. chew   c. fly

4. one   d. floor

Activity 2

Circle the correctly spelled word.

1. A diamond/diemund is a jewel.

2. A nife/knife is used to cut bread.

3. The state of Hawaii is made up of many islands/ilands.

4. You shud/should look both ways before crossing the street.

Activity 3

Read the words in the box.

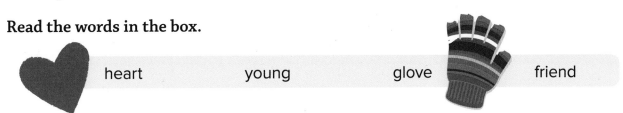

| heart | young | glove | friend |

Circle the word that is misspelled even though it looks like it sounds. Then find the right spelling of the word in the box. Write it at the end of the sentence.

1. Jamie lost her gluv on the way home. _____

2. Ira drew a picture in the shape of a hart. _____

3. Tara's mother said she was too yung to stay up late. _____

4. Renaldo's best frend taught him how to swim. _____

Activity 4

1. Circle the words that are not spelled the way they sound.

free	know
iron	eighty
hi	captain
knock	clap
dough	fifty

2. Pick two words from the list above and write a sentence for each.

_____

_____

Fluency: Read with Purpose and Understanding

In this section, you will work with an adult as you practice and develop the art of fluent reading. Fluency means reading with speed, accuracy, and proper expression.

Fluency provides a connection between recognizing and understanding words. When reading to themselves, fluent readers will group words together so that they recognize them right away. When reading aloud, they have a naturalness to their reading and speak with expression.

Whether you are a fluent reader already or are working toward this goal, keep practicing so that you will continue to grow in your reading abilities.

We hope you enjoy reviewing these important skills as you progress through your Common Core journey to excellence.

Let's practice!

Standards RF.2.4.a, RF.2.4.b, RF.2.4.c

Adults:

While your student is reading aloud, time him or her for one minute and mark any words that are missed by writing them down or crossing them out. When you get to one minute, note how far the student has read, but allow him or her to continue the story. Count the total number of errors made during one minute and subtract that from the number of words read during that minute. This will give you the total number of words read per minute.

TOTAL NUMBER OF WORDS – NUMBER OF ERRORS = WORDS READ PER MINUTE

Over an extended period of time, your student's fluency should increase by the number of words read per minute.

Unit 1 (September)	Unit 2 (December)	Unit 3 (March)	Unit 4 (June)
50	60	70	90

Science at the Park

Jaquan is at a summer science camp. He has written a letter to his brother, Terrell, to share what he is doing at camp.

Dear Terrell,   2

Summer science camp is really cool. We are learning about science and still having   16
lots of fun. My group leader's name is Rachel. This week, we learned how to do   32
science experiments in our own backyard or at a nearby park.   43

Our first activity was called What's in a Circle? We placed hula-hoops on a big   58
space in the field. Then, we looked very carefully at the ground to see what was   74
inside our own hula-hoop. Rachel helped me to look through a big glass. It helped   89
me to see the ground more closely. I saw ants and other small flowers. I also   105
learned that there are lots of different insects and plants that can live together   119
in one area. I discovered some other insects, but I didn't know their names.   133

The next day, we met our **field guide**. A field guide likes to help other people   149
understand nature. Our field guide helped us name some of the living things that   163
we discovered in our hula-hoops. Bees also live near the same area with the ants   178
and flowers. Our guide told us that we must be careful so that the bees do not   195
sting us.   197

I can't believe summer camp is almost over! Rachel has invited all the students to   212
come back for one weekend in the fall. Then, we are going to look at those same   229
areas and see how they are different as the season changes. Rachel says that   243
we will be able to watch caterpillars munch on fall leaves! Doesn't that sound   257
exciting? I can't wait to tell you more about it when I come home!   271

Sincerely, Jaquan   273

**Words read in
1 minute – errors = WPM**

Standards RF.2.4.a, RF.2.4.b, RF.2.4.c

CHECK FOR UNDERSTANDING

Adults: After your student has finished reading, ask him or her to provide a brief summary of the letter. This will let you know if he or she understood what was read. Write what your student says on the lines below.

_____

_____

_____

GUIDED QUESTIONS

Use "Science at the Park" to answer the following questions.

1. Name two places that kids can study science.

   _____

   _____

2. Reread paragraph 3. What is a **field guide**?

   _____

   _____

3. Explain why Rachel has invited the students back to study during the fall.

   _____

   _____

4. Reread these sentences with expression.

   "Doesn't that sound exciting? I can't wait to tell you more about it when I come home!"

   Based on these two sentences, how does Jaquan feel about summer science camp? Explain your answer in your own words.

   _____

   _____

Sparky the Guide Dog

"Ruff, Ruff!" barked our four-legged friend.	6
"What's the matter?" yelled Dad from the kitchen.	14
"Nothing, Dad! There's a box in front of the staircase. Annabelle and Sparky are	28
trying to go upstairs, so I'll move it."	36
"Thanks, Jeremy!" replied Dad.	40
Our family dog is pretty special. His name is Sparky. My older sister Annabelle	54
needs Sparky the most, but everyone in our home loves him. Sparky is a guide dog. Dad	71
brought Sparky home to help Annabelle because she cannot see on her own. Guide dogs	86
are trained to help people who are blind, like Annabelle. There was a lot more I wanted	103
to know about Sparky, so I asked Dad.	111
"Dad?"	112
"Yes, Jeremy?"	114
"How does Sparky know to bark when something is in the way?"	126
"Well, son, Sparky was trained before he came to our home to help Annabelle. He is	142
able to stop at the top and bottom of stairs. Sparky is also able to stay away from many	161
things that could be dangerous for Annabelle. Your sister actually does a lot of the	176
guiding, too. They really have to know each other."	185
"Why do guide dogs follow orders?"	191
"Guide dogs are **trained** to follow their handlers' instructions. So if Annabelle and	204
Sparky are crossing the street, Sparky listens to Annabelle if she gives him the OK to	220
cross. However, if there is any danger, Sparky will not move."	231
"Our neighbors like to pet Sparky and offer him treats."	241
"Why doesn't he eat them?"	246
"Sometimes he does, but Sparky does not always take treats	256
or like to be petted. Sparky does not like to lose focus because his	270
number one job is to help Annabelle get from place to place."	282
"Wow!" I replied. "That's pretty amazing, Dad!"	289
Sparky the guide dog has a very important job. I knew he	301
was great, but knowing what he really does makes me love	312
Sparky even more.	315

Words read in 1 minute – errors = WPM

Standards RF.2.4.a, RF.2.4.b, RF.2.4.c

CHECK FOR UNDERSTANDING

Adults: After your student has finished reading, ask him or her to provide a brief summary of the story. This will let you know if he or she understood what was read. Write what your student says on the lines below.

_____

_____

_____

GUIDED QUESTIONS

Use "Sparky the Guide Dog" to answer the following questions.

1. Why does Annabelle need Sparky?

_____

_____

2. Reread this sentence from the passage:

   *"Guide dogs are **trained** to follow their handlers' instructions."*

   Using the context clues in the sentence, what does the word **trained** mean?

_____

_____

3. Explain how Sparky might react to a dangerous situation.

_____

_____

4. Why does Sparky turn down treats?

_____

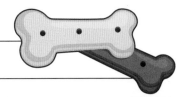

_____

Let's Recycle!

Did you know that Americans use 2,500,000 plastic bottles every hour? Many of these	14
bottles are thrown in the trash. That's a lot of plastic! These plastic bottles aren't good	30
for the environment. Many times, they simply sit in a landfill or float into the ocean,	46
where they can last for thousands of years. This can be harmful to animals in the water	63
because the bottles take up too much of their natural space.	74

Is there a way to save the planet from unwanted trash?   85
One answer is *recycling*. Recycling means using old materials   94
to make new products. For example, if you drink a juice and   106
recycle the box, the box can be turned into a new box that   119
can store more juice. This process is seen in this symbol—a   131
recycling loop.   133

Notice that there are three arrows. Each arrow stands for a step in the recycling   148
process.   149

1. The first step is collection. Old materials are picked up through programs or   163
   large storage areas.   166
2. The second step is processing. New materials are made from the old materials.   180
3. The last step is purchasing. People buy the recycled products.   191

Recycling also helps save energy. If each American recycled every single can he or she   206
used for one whole year, it would save enough energy to light the city of Washington,   222
D.C. for almost four years!   227

Here is a list of common items you can recycle: 237
• Glass bottles   239
• Plastic containers   241
• Aluminum food cans and other metals   247
• Cardboard   248
When recycled, these materials are used to make new   257
products such as playground equipment, containers, drinking   264
water bottles, and even the steel in skyscrapers.   272

To find out more about recycling or how you can help, visit this website: 286
www.ecy.wa.gov.   287

Words read in 1 minute – errors = WPM

CHECK FOR UNDERSTANDING

Adults: After your student has finished reading, ask him or her to provide a brief summary of the text. This will let you know if he or she understood what was read. Write what your student says on the lines below.

_____

_____

_____

GUIDED QUESTIONS

Use "Let's Recycle!" to answer the following questions.

1. Why is unwanted trash bad for the Earth?

   _____

   _____

2. Reread this sentence from the article.

   "Did you know that Americans use 2,500,000 plastic bottles every hour?"

   Which answer **best** describes how many plastic bottles Americans use daily?

   A. only a few   B. very many   C. not enough

3. Explain the three steps in the recycling process.

   _____

   _____

4. According to the author, what can you do to find out more information about how you can help to recycle?

   _____

   _____

How to Paper Mâché

Have you ever seen a colorful piece of art? Arts and crafts can be great fun! Making art	18
can also help you to learn about different colors, shapes, and materials.	30
Today, you are the artist! You will learn how to paper mâché [paper ma-SHAY].	44
The name "paper mâché" comes from French words that mean "chewed paper."	56
In this type of art project, an object is covered in paper using glue or a	72
pasty mixture. After that, the object is decorated.	80

Here is what you will need: 86

For the Paper Mâché Mixture	91	**For the Artwork**	111
1 cup of flour	95	strips of newspaper	114
1 cup of water	99	paper towels	116
large mixing bowl or tray	104	white or colored construction paper	121
large spoon	106	paint brush	123
salt (optional)	108	crayons, markers, colored pencils, or paint	129
		any object to paper mâché (ball, toy, bowl,	137
		or box)	139

Directions for the mixture: 143

Mix the flour and the water in a large mixing bowl. Stir them together with a large	160
spoon until the mixture looks like glue. If it is too thick, add more water. Be sure the	178
mixture doesn't have any lumps! If you plan on saving some of the mixture and using	194
it for other projects, add a spoonful of salt so that it doesn't mold.	208

Now that your mixture is ready, begin creating your masterpiece! 218

1. First, decide what object you want to use.	227
2. Then soak the strips of newspaper in the mixture.	237
3. Next, cover your object completely with the soaked newspaper strips.	248
4. Let the first layer dry. Then, add two or three more layers and let them dry.	265
5. Add a final layer of plain or colored construction paper to the object.	279
Smooth down the edges of the paper with glue and a paintbrush. Let dry.	293
6. Finally, decorate your object using crayons, markers, colored pencils, or paint.	305
Ta-dah! Now you know how to paper mâché. You can show off your lovely artwork,	320
or even try teaching what you have learned to a friend or family member.	334

Words read in 1 minute — errors = WPM

Standards RF.2.4.a, RF.2.4.b, RF.2.4.c

CHECK FOR UNDERSTANDING

Adults: After your student has finished reading, ask him or her to provide a brief summary of the text. This will let you know if he or she understood what was being read. Write what your student says on the lines below.

_____

_____

_____

GUIDED QUESTIONS

Use **"How to Paper Mâché"** to answer the following questions.

1. According to the author, what is one good thing about art?

   _____

   _____

2. Reread this sentence.

   "You will learn how to **paper mâché***."*

   What do the words **paper mâché** mean?

   _____

   _____

3. Why are there two separate lists of things you need for paper mâché projects?

   _____

   _____

4. What does the author use to teach you how to paper mâché?

   _____

   _____

Reading and Writing:
Informational Texts

How Flowers and Plants Grow

In this unit you will learn about a plant's life cycle and what it needs to grow and make new plants. You will also learn the parts of a flower and the important jobs that each part has.

Plants are very important for life on Earth. They give people and animals oxygen to breathe and food to eat. They also make the Earth look pretty.

Happy reading!

Amazing Plants

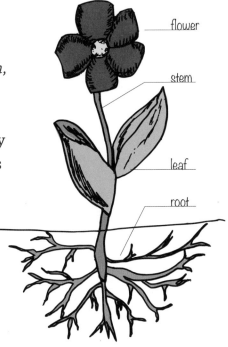

flower

stem

leaf

root

1 Plants are living things that are an important part of our world. They come from tiny seeds that grow when conditions are right. Plants have four main parts that help them grow: the *roots, stem, leaves*, and *flower*.

2 Did you know that the most important part of a plant is hidden underground? The roots are important to a plant's ability to grow and reproduce. They hold the plant in the ground. Roots take in water and other **nutrients** from the soil.

3 The water and the nutrients are moved from the roots up through the stem of the plant. The stem then carries the nutrients to the different parts of the plant. It is also the part of the plant that helps it stand tall and strong. Some plants' stems are thick and woody, like the trunk of a tree. Other plants' stems are soft and thin, like the stem of a flower.

4 Water and other nutrients help plants stay healthy. However, plants are also able to make their own food. The leaves of a plant use air, water, and the sun to make food. The food travels through the stem to the rest of the plant. Some of the nutrients are stored within the leaves to make sure the plant has enough **energy** to grow and live.

5 The flower of a plant plays an important part in helping plants continue to grow and live. The basic parts of a flower are the *petals*, the *pistil*, and the *stamen*. The pistil and the stamen are the parts that allow the plant to grow new plants. They are surrounded by the petals.

Each part of a plant has a special job to do. If any one of these parts does not do its job, the plant would not be able to grow.

Digging Deeper

Adults, you can help your student watch the way plants take in their water and other nutrients by trying this simple experiment.

Students, you will need: celery, clear cup, water, and food color (dark blue or red)

Experiment: Fill a clear plastic cup with tap water. Put 2–5 drops of food coloring in the water. Take a stalk of celery and cut the end off to allow for freshness. Place it in the water, and in about an hour you will see the color rising up the stalk! When you have completed the experiment, tell a friend what happened to the celery.

FINDING THE MAIN IDEA AND DETAILS

Use "Amazing Plants" to answer the following questions.

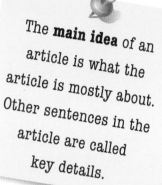

The **main idea** of an article is what the article is mostly about. Other sentences in the article are called key details.

1. What is the **main idea** of the passage?

   A. Plants have different parts that help them grow.

   B. Roots are important in helping a plant grow.

   C. Leaves take in sun and air to help the plant grow.

2. Circle the sentence that contains the **best** key detail for the main idea of the passage.

   A. Each part of the plant has a special job to do.

   B. Roots hold the plant in the ground.

   C. Flowers help make new plants.

3. What is the **main idea** of the third paragraph?

   A. The stem of the plant helps it stand tall and strong.

   B. The stem carries nutrients to different parts of the plant.

   C. The stem does many important jobs within the plant.

4. Select a **key detail** for the main idea of the third paragraph.

   A. The stem carries nutrients to different parts of the plant.

   B. Water and other nutrients help plants stay healthy.

   C. Some plants' stems are thick and woody.

A **key detail** is a sentence that tells about the main idea!

DESCRIBING SCIENTIFIC IDEAS

When we read information about a concept in science, it helps to describe the connections between and within the scientific concepts. Studying the information helps us to better understand the ideas behind it.

After reading the article "Amazing Plants," use the template below to write each plant part and its job.

Plant Part	Plant Job

UNDERSTANDING THE CLUES

When you are not sure of the meaning of a word, you can use context clues. **Context clues** are clues within the text that help you determine the meaning of an unknown word. You can use other words around the unknown word to help you find the meaning.

1. Reread the following sentence from the article.

   *"Water and other **nutrients** help plants stay healthy."*

   What does the word **nutrients** mean?
   - A. ingredients
   - B. minerals
   - C. leaves

2. Think about yourself. What types of nutrients does your body need to be healthy?

   _____

3. Reread the following sentence from the article.

   *"Some of the nutrients are stored within the leaves to make sure the plant has enough **energy** to grow and live."*

   What does the word **energy** mean?
   - A. light
   - B. help
   - C. power

4. Think about yourself. Why is it important for your body to store and use **energy**?

   _____

USING NOUNS AND ADJECTIVES

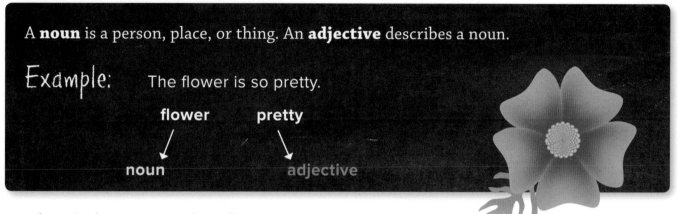

A **noun** is a person, place, or thing. An **adjective** describes a noun.

Example: The flower is so pretty.

flower   pretty

↓   ↓

noun   adjective

1. Identify the **nouns** in the following sentence and write them below.

    "Some plants' stems are thick and woody, like the trunk of a tree."

    _____

2. Identify the **adjectives** in the following sentence and write them below.

    "Other plants' stems are soft and thin, like the stem of a flower."

    _____

3. Which of the following words is **not** a noun?

    A. water

    B. grow

    C. roots

4. Which of the following words is **not** an adjective?

    A. trunk

    B. thick

    C. woody

WRITE YOUR OPINION

Imagine you are looking at a beautiful flower that is almost ready to grow fruit. Suddenly, another child comes along to pick it.

Write an opinion essay about why you think the child should let the flower continue to grow and complete the cycle of life. Be sure your essay has a topic sentence (or main idea) that tells your opinion. Next, list three reasons why the child should let the flower grow. Finally, write a conclusion that retells your opinion.

Use the graphic organizer below to help plan your essay.

Topic Sentence: Stop—Don't pick that flower!

Reason 1:

Reason 2:

Reason 3:

Conclusion: What will you choose to do?

WRITE YOUR ESSAY

Use your outline from page 42 to develop your work below. Plan an introduction, a body with your facts, and a conclusion.

Introduction: _____

_____

_____

_____

_____

_____

Body: _____

_____

_____

_____

_____

_____

_____

_____

_____

_____

Conclusion: _____

_____

_____

_____

_____

_____

_____

The Cycle of Life

1   How a plant goes from being a seed to a full-grown plant is known as its life cycle. Like most other living things, plants start out small and grow bigger.

2   Plants can make new plants in several ways. This is called **reproduction**. Plants reproduce using seeds and **pollen**. A plant that uses seeds to reproduce often does this through its fruit. Usually, a flower blossoms on the plant and begins to fall off when the fruit starts growing. The fruit continues to grow and change until it is fully **ripe**. If it does not get picked and eaten by a human or an animal, the fruit falls off the plant. As the fruit rots on the ground, the seeds inside are freed. Sunlight, soil, water, and air help bury the seeds in the ground. Each seed has a small plant inside of it that can begin to grow if conditions are right. The seed also contains food that feeds the plant until it sprouts. Once a seed sprouts, it grows into a seedling, or young plant. Seedlings grow into adult plants, and the life cycle starts all over again.

3   Plants that use pollen to reproduce also need help from insects. First, a plant produces a flower. The bright colors of the flower draw insects to it. When an insect lands on the flower, pollen sticks to the insect's feet. When the insect leaves, it carries the pollen to a different plant. When the insect lands on the new plant's flower, the pollen from the first plant falls off of the insect's body into the flower. Once the flower has the pollen, it can start making seeds for new plants.

4   Some plants with flowers use the wind to **spread** their pollen. These plants are almost always dark in color. They make large amounts of pollen so that some of it will hopefully reach another

glossary

Pollen: Yellow dust that is produced by a plant and that is carried to other plants of the same kind usually by wind or insects so that the plants can produce seeds

Reproduction: The process that produces babies, young animals, or new plants

Ripe: Completely grown and ready to be eaten

plant. When the wind blows, it carries the pollen off the plant, into the air, and then onto a second plant. The second plant uses the pollen to make new seeds. Finally, a new plant can start to grow. Each time a new plant grows, the life cycle of the plant begins again.

FINDING THE MAIN IDEA AND DETAILS

Use "The Cycle of Life" to answer the following questions.

1. What is the **main idea** of the article?

   A. Flowers need insects to help them grow.
   B. Wind spreads pollen to help plants grow.
   C. Plants have several ways to grow new plants.

2. What is the **best** key detail that supports the main idea of the article?

   A. Fruit holds the seeds for the plant.
   B. Some plants make large amounts of pollen.
   C. Plants use seeds and pollen to grow new plants.

3. Explain why some plants need insects.

   _____

   _____

   _____

4. Explain the steps a seed must go through to become a new plant. Be sure to write your answer in complete sentences.

   _____

   _____

   _____

VOCABULARY DEVELOPMENT

You can figure out the meaning of a word by looking at the clues. The words around the word you do not know can help you figure out its meaning.

Use "The Cycle of Life" to answer the following questions.

1. Which sentence uses the word **sticks** the same way as the sentence below?

   *"When an insect lands on the flower, pollen **sticks** to the insect's feet."*

   A.   The boys picked up many sticks before raking leaves in their yard.

   B.   "Be sure to throw away your popsicle sticks," said Mom.

   C.   A frog uses its feet when it sticks to a tree.

2. Which sentence uses the word **land** the same way as the sentence below?

   *"When the insect **lands** on the new plant's flower, the pollen from the first plant falls off of the insect's body into the flower."*

   A.   The plane was able to land smoothly on the runway.

   B.   The class marked the outline of the land they were studying.

   C.   The sailor yelled to his crew when he spotted dry land.

SHADES OF MEANING

3. Which word is closely related to **bright**?

   A.   gloomy

   B.   brilliant

   C.   dull

4. Which word is closely related to **spread**?

   A.   scatter

   B.   spring

   C.   spray

Standards RI.2.4, L.2.5.b

COMPARING AND CONTRASTING ARTICLES

After reading "Amazing Plants" and "The Cycle of Life," describe how the articles are similar and different. Fill in the Venn diagram below.

Amazing Plants (different)

The Cycle of Life (different)

WRITE YOUR EXPLANATION

You are going to present a report to your class. You have chosen the topic of how plants reproduce. Using evidence from the text as well as additional research, think of organizing your material in a nice way to help your classmates understand this wonderful process. Gather your facts, and supporting evidence for each fact. Use the organizer that follows to help build your outline.

Introduction (Clearly state your topic):

_____

Fact 1 (Supporting detail):

_____

_____

_____

Fact 2 (Supporting detail):

_____

_____

_____

Fact 3 (Supporting detail):

_____

_____

_____

Conclusion:

_____

Remember to use your *My Journal* pages at the back of the workbook if you need more space to write.

Animals With and Without Backbones

Animals that are similar in important ways are divided into groups, or classes. Every animal in the world belongs to a class. The five most well-known classes of animals with backbones are mammals, birds, fish, reptiles, and amphibians. There are also many animals without backbones. Two of the most common classes are spiders and insects.

Bony

1 Did you know that not all animals have backbones? In fact, the animals that do have backbones are only a small group compared to the total number of animals in the world. Animals with backbones are called vertebrates. All vertebrates have a skeleton and muscles. They also have eyes in the front of their bodies. Some types of vertebrates include mammals, fish, and reptiles.

2 Mammals are the smartest and most well-known group of vertebrates. You are a mammal. Mammals are warm-blooded, which means they always keep the same body temperature. All mammals have hair or fur. This is one way they can live in both cold and warm weather. Most mammals give birth to live babies. They are the only vertebrates that feed their babies milk.

3 Fish are the largest group of vertebrates. Fish are cold-blooded animals. Their body temperature can be cold or warm, depending on the temperature of the water. Fish are covered in scales. Scientists can tell the age of a fish by looking at its scales. A fish's scales are covered in a special slime that helps it move through the water. Fish breathe by taking air out of the water through their gills. Fish do not have feet, but they do have fins. They use their fins to stay upright and move through the water.

4 Reptiles are also cold-blooded vertebrates. They can live on land or in the water. When reptiles need to get warm, they go out in the sun. When they need to cool down, they lie in the shade. Reptiles are covered in scales that protect their bodies from losing too much water through their skin. Reptile scales can be large or small and of many colors. Most reptiles have four legs and a tail. Snakes and some lizards are the only land vertebrates that do not have legs. Many kinds of reptiles lay eggs and then **abandon** them to hatch on their own.

5 Vertebrates are very smart animals that can adapt, or change, according to where they live. They have been alive on Earth for millions of years. It is hard to believe they make up such a small part of all living things!

Digging Deeper

If you are interested in learning more about vertebrates, go to the following website and watch this simple slide show. studyjams.scholastic.com/studyjams/jams/science/animals/vertebrates.html

FINDING THE MAIN IDEA AND DETAILS

Use "Bony" to answer the following questions.

1. What is the **main idea** of the article?

    A. Mammals are the most well-known vertebrates.

    B. Reptiles are also cold-blooded vertebrates.

    C. Animals with backbones are called vertebrates.

2. Which sentence provides the best **key detail** for the main idea of the article?

    A. Mammals are the only vertebrates that feed their babies milk.

    B. Scales protect reptiles from losing too much water through their skin.

    C. All vertebrates have a skeleton and muscles.

> The **main idea** of an article is what the text is mostly about. The **key details** support the main idea.

AUTHOR'S PURPOSE

3. What was the **author's purpose** in writing the article?

    A. To talk about his or her favorite kinds of vertebrates.

    B. To give information about the different kinds of vertebrates.

    C. To give an opinion about the different kinds of vertebrates.

> Sometimes an author will want to entertain a reader. Other times he or she may want to teach a reader more information. An article can also be written to convince a reader to believe a certain topic or opinion.

USING PAST TENSE VERBS

The **past tense** of a verb shows that an action has already happened. Simply add -ed to the present tense verb in order to change it to past tense.

prance   ---->   pranced

walk   ---->   walked

Linking verbs do not express action, but they do connect the subject of the verb to the additional information about the subject.

Example: Rashaun **is** painting a picture of his favorite bird.

When you are changing a verb from present to past tense, you will also need to drop the linking verb before changing the ending of a verb to make it past tense.

is painting ---->   is painted ---->   painted

Irregular verbs do not follow the simple pattern of adding an -ed to the end of the word. Spelling can be tricky for these types of verbs. While some irregular verbs only change one letter, others have several letters that change. Memorizing is a great way to learn irregular verbs.

feed   ---->   fed

fly   ---->   flew

hold   ---->   held

spring   ---->   sprang

USING PAST TENSE VERBS

1. Choose the sentence written with a past tense verb.

   A. The lizard found a sunny spot.

   B. The frog lays eggs in the water.

   C. The fish will swim up river in the spring.

2. Change the highlighted word in the sentence to the past tense.

   The lion **hides** her babies in the tall grass. Past tense: _____.

   The mouse **runs** away from the alligator. Past tense: _____.

3. Change the following verbs from present tense to past tense.

   sit _____

   eat _____

   tell _____

USING ADVERBS

An adverb tells when, where, or how something happened. Adverbs often end in -ly, such as *quietly* or *peacefully*.

Choose an adverb from the word bank to complete each sentence.

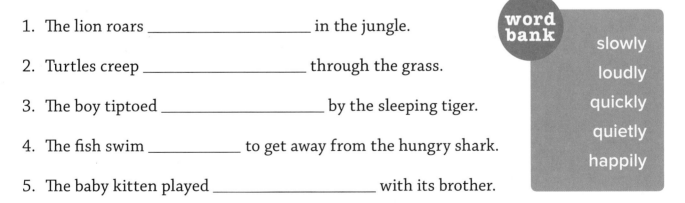

1. The lion roars _____ in the jungle.

2. Turtles creep _____ through the grass.

3. The boy tiptoed _____ by the sleeping tiger.

4. The fish swim _____ to get away from the hungry shark.

5. The baby kitten played _____ with its brother.

word bank

slowly

loudly

quickly

quietly

happily

PREFIXES

A **prefix** is a group of letters added to the beginning of a word to create a new word. For example, **re** means again and **un** means not.

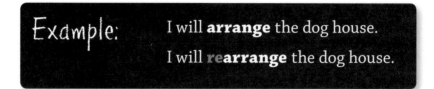

Example: I will **arrange** the dog house.

I will **rearrange** the dog house.

Create a new word by adding a prefix to each highlighted word. Then tell what the new word means.

1. What is the new meaning of the word **happy** when the prefix **un-** is added?

   New word: _____   Meaning: _____

2. What is the new meaning of the word **write** when the prefix **re-** is added?

   New word: _____   Meaning: _____

SHADES OF MEANING

Many verbs and adjectives are closely related to one another. They have similar definitions, but have slightly different meanings. Some words are stronger or weaker in meaning.

Look at the verbs in each sentence. How does the meaning of the sentence change with the use of the different verbs? Select a definition from the right that gives the correct meaning to each sentence. Use a dictionary if you need help. Write the letter of the meaning next to each sentence. Then, answer questions 4 and 5.

glossary

1. Reptiles **abandon** their eggs to hatch on their own. _____

2. Reptiles **leave** their eggs to hatch on their own. _____

3. Reptiles **discard** their eggs to hatch on their own. _____

4. Which verb has the *strongest* meaning? _____

5. Which verb has the *weakest* meaning? _____

A: To go out or away from the eggs

B: To give up the eggs completely

C: To get rid of the eggs as something useless or unwanted

Spineless

1 Stop and think about what life would be like without a backbone or a spine. Animals that do not have a backbone are called *invertebrates* (in-vur-tuh-brits). Some well-known kinds of invertebrates are arthropods, sponges, and earthworms.

2 Arthropods are the biggest group of invertebrates in the world. Arthropods include insects, spiders, centipedes, and lobsters. These animals have bodies that are broken into sections called **segments**.

3 They also have jointed legs that bend and move just like our knees and elbows do. Each arthropod has a hard outer shell on its body called an exoskeleton (ek-so-skel-i-ton). This shell has a very important job: it protects the animal inside!

4 Sponges are another kind of invertebrate. They are one of the smallest animal groups in the ocean. Sponges do not have legs or any way to move, so they stay in one place for their whole lives. Sponges take in food from the water through hollow tubes with many openings called pores. Even though sponges do not have many **enemies**, they do have a way to protect themselves. Sponges can give off toxins into the water around them that kill anything trying to harm them. People have found ways to use some of these **toxins** in medicines.

5 Have you ever seen worms all over the ground after a rainstorm? These are earthworms, another kind of invertebrate. Earthworms have no arms, legs, or eyes. Instead, they have many segments in their bodies. The number of segments earthworms have depends on how much they eat. If they have a lot to eat, they have more segments. If they do not have a lot to eat, they have fewer segments. Earthworms are also very important to plants and gardens. They eat dead things in the ground, and their waste helps plants grow.

6 These are just a few of the many kinds of invertebrates. Even though some are slow-moving and small, almost ninety-eight percent of all animals in the world are invertebrates!

Digging Deeper

With help from an adult, go outside and find some fresh dirt. Using a shovel, gently dig down a little bit and turn over the dirt. See if you can find an earthworm! If you can't find any in your yard, try looking online to find a picture of an earthworm under a microscope! Draw a picture of the worms you find!

glossary

Enemies: Animals that harm other animals

Segment: Section

Toxin: A substance that is poisonous

FINDING THE MAIN IDEA AND DETAILS

Use "Spineless" to answer the following questions.

1. What is the **main idea** of the article?

    A. Earthworms are important to plants.
    B. Arthropods are the largest group of invertebrates.
    C. Animals that do not have backbones are called invertebrates.

2. Which sentence provides the best **key detail** for the main idea of the article?

    A. Arthropods have exoskeletons that protect them.
    B. Sponges do not have legs and stay in one place their whole lives.
    C. The number of segments earthworms have depends on how much they eat.

3. What does the author explain in paragraph 2?

    A. Why arthropods have knees like people.
    B. Some special features of arthropods.
    C. How arthropods are like other invertebrates.

4. What is the main idea of paragraph 4?

    A. Sponges take in food from the water through hollow tubes.
    B. Sponges are a small group of invertebrates that live in the ocean.
    C. People make medicine from sponges' toxins.

Standards RI.2.1, RI.2.2

USING REFERENCE MATERIAL

Look at the dictionary items below. These are words from the article "Spineless." After reading the dictionary words and phrases, answer the questions below.

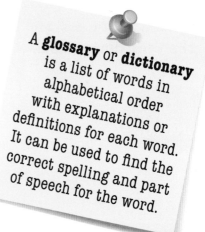

A **glossary** or **dictionary** is a list of words in alphabetical order with explanations or definitions for each word. It can be used to find the correct spelling and part of speech for the word.

backbone (bak-bohn) noun
    1. The spinal column; spine

jointed (join-tid) adjective
    1. Having joints
    2. Formed with knots

hollow (hol-oh) adjective
    1. Having a space or a cavity inside; not solid; empty
    2. Having a hole that curves inward

segments (seg-ment) noun
    1. Zoology
        a. Any of the rings that make up the body of some kinds of invertebrates such as an arthropod
        b. Any of the separate parts of the body of an animal, especially of an arthropod

1. Something that has an empty space is called _____.

    A. hallow

    B. hollow

    C. haulo

2. A spine is also called a _____.

    A. buckbone

    B. backbone

    C. breakbone

COMPARING AND CONTRASTING ARTICLES

After reading "Spineless" and "Bony," describe how the articles are similar and different. Fill in the Venn diagram below.

Spineless (different)

Similar

Bony (different)

Standard RI.2.9

USING APOSTROPHES

A *contraction* is formed when you combine two words to make a new word with an apostrophe (for example, *can* + *not* = **can't**). A *possessive noun* is a noun that uses an apostrophe to show possession, or ownership (for example, "*That is the **dog's** bone.*")

Activity 1

Read the sentences from the article and change the bolded words into a contraction.

1. Animals that **do not** have a backbone are called invertebrates. _____

2. **They are** one of the smallest animal groups in the ocean. _____

3. An invertebrate has a body **that is** broken into sections called segments. _____

Activity 2

Read the following sentences. Place an apostrophe on the bolded word to form a possessive noun.

1. The **lobsters** body is broken into segments.

2. A **sponges** toxin protects it from predators.

3. An **earthworms** segments are affected by how much food it eats.

WRITE TO GIVE INFORMATION

When you are asked to write an informative writing piece, you will need to do a little research on the topic.

By reading "Spineless," you have learned about different kinds of invertebrates. With help from an adult, research a few more types of invertebrates. Write down the name of one you find interesting.

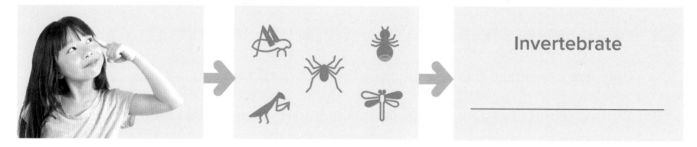

Invertebrate

_____

Now, choose an invertebrate you want to write about. Gather your information and facts. Use the organizer below to plan your writing.

The invertebrate I chose to write about is _____

Fact 1:
Fact 2:
Fact 3:
Fact 4:
Fact 5:

Remember to use your *My Journal* pages at the back of the workbook if you need more space to write.

WRITE YOUR ESSAY

Use your outline from page 60 to develop your work below. Plan an introduction, a body with your facts, and a conclusion. If you want to include a drawing or diagram of your invertebrate, place it in the section with your facts.

Introduce your topic: _____

_____

_____

_____

_____

_____

Use facts and definitions to develop your story and include drawings or diagrams:

_____

_____

_____

_____

_____

_____

_____

_____

_____

Write your conclusion: _____

_____

_____

_____

_____

_____

_____

Congratulations! You have completed the lessons in this section. Now you will have the opportunity to practice some of the skills you just learned.

Reading Fluency

Adults: Time your student for one minute while he or she reads to you. Use the numbers on the right-hand margin to determine how many words the student has read after one minute. Keep track of the number of errors the student makes while reading. (Your student should be able to read 60–90 words per minute.) Have your student continue reading to the end of the article and then answer the questions that follow.

Meet the Marine Iguana

Adult marine iguanas are excellent swimmers. They glide through the water easily. They	13
dive under the water to get seaweed and algae to eat. They can hold their breath for longer	31
than an hour. When on land, they do not move as quickly. It is harder for them to get	50
around. Because marine iguanas are cold-blooded, when they leave the water they must	63
huddle together for warmth on sunny rocks. When they are hot, they lift themselves up	78
from the rock to feel the breeze under their bodies.	88
Marine iguanas only live on special islands off the coast of South America. They are	103
in danger. Tourists coming from all over the world bring new germs to the islands. The	120
iguanas are not strong enough to fight off the new diseases. Their population has been	134
going down for years. Laws have been set up to protect the iguanas.	147

Words read in 1 minute – errors = WPM

Standard RF.4.b

Activity 1

Use what you know about verbs to change the following verbs from present tense to past tense.

1. swim _____
2. hold _____
3. crawl _____

Activity 2

Read the passage. Then choose an adverb to complete the sentences below.

word bank closely quickly slowly

1. Iguanas swim _____ through the water.
2. Iguanas huddle together _____ to keep warm.
3. When on land, iguanas move around very _____.

Activity 3

Add in the proper punctuation to the bolded words in each sentence.

1. A **lizards** food is usually found on land.
2. The **iguanas** tail moves so it can swim in the water.
3. The **tourists** hat flew in the wind and landed on the iguana's head.

Activity 4

Use what you know about closely related adjectives to complete the story below. Fill in each blank with the correct word.

word bank grand   huge   big   great

My friend Vito has a pet gecko named Lumpkins. It has grown so much in the last month. Vito had to buy another cage because Lumpkins became too _____ for the one he had. Lumpkins loves to eat. He has a _____ appetite. He can eat ten worms in one meal! When we take Lumpkins out of the cage, he gets very happy. We enjoy playing with him because he has a _____ personality. Lumpkins likes to play on the hamster wheel. Sometimes he puts on a _____ show and runs on the wheel at lightning speed!

Let's apply the reading skills you covered in this section.

Jumping Spiders

When you think of a spider, do you think of a creature that spins webs? Most people do. But did you know that not all spiders use their silk to make webs? Some spiders are very different from others. One such spider is the jumping spider.

You might be wondering, if jumping spiders do not spin webs, how do they catch food? First, they have very good eyesight that helps them be **effective** hunters. They have two large eyes at the front of their head and three smaller eyes on each side. Other spiders that use webs to catch their **prey** have very poor eyesight. Second, jumping spiders jump onto their prey to catch it. In fact, they can leap from ten to forty times their body length!

Another **trait** that makes jumping spiders different from other spiders is their color. Most spiders are darker in color. But not jumping spiders! They are very colorful. Male jumping spiders also have special traits such as patches of hair on their legs.

However, like other spiders, jumping spiders use their silk to protect their eggs by making a silk bed and blanket. Both jumping spiders and other spiders use their silk as a safety line if they happen to fall.

So before you decide to step on the next spider you see, think about the jumping spider, an amazing and **unique** creature.

glossary

Effective: Able to produce the desired result

Trait: A distinguishing feature or quality

Prey: An animal hunted for food

Unique: Very unusual

Use "Jumping Spiders" to answer the following questions.

1. Reread the following sentence from the article.

    *"Both jumping spiders and other spiders use their silk as a **safety line** <u>if they happen to fall</u>."*

    What is the meaning of **safety line**? Use the underlined word clues to figure out the meaning.

    _____

2. Which word from the article is a context clue for the meaning of the word **leap**?
    A. catch
    B. jump
    C. protect

3. What is the **main idea** of the article?

    A. Jumping spiders do not spin webs.
    B. Jumping spiders use their silk in different ways.
    C. Jumping spiders have traits that make them different from other spiders.

4. Which **key detail** supports the main idea of the article?
    A. Jumping spiders leap on their prey to catch it.
    B. Jumping spiders make silk beds and blankets for their eggs.
    C. Jumping spiders use their silk as a safety line if they happen to fall.

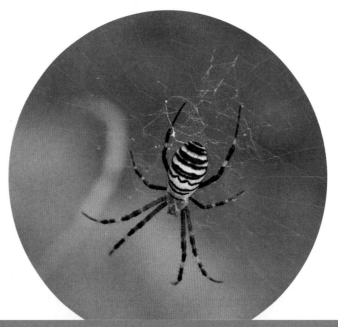

DISCOVER

What would you say? Let's take what you have learned and write about it!

Share Your Opinion

Your class is going to get a pet. The choices are a fish, a lizard, a hamster, or a ferret. Your teacher wants a letter from you and each of your classmates stating your opinion. You must decide what kind of pet the class should get and list the reasons why. Which animal would you recommend? Which animal do you think would make the best class pet, and why?

Using the organizer below, plan out your letter. Do research about the animal you have chosen. With the help of an adult, use the Internet to conduct your search. Or you may use other books in your home or at your local library. Be sure to list reasons that support your opinion.

My opinion is: _____

The reason(s) I think (**your opinion**) is because (**list a reason**): _____

_____

Supporting detail: _____

_____

_____

Supporting detail: _____

_____

_____

Conclusion: _____

_____

_____

_____

Share Your Opinion

Now that you have a plan for your writing, use the information from your graphic organizer to write out your opinion. Include **_linking words_** in your letter. Also called connecting words, linking words connect thoughts and ideas. You can use the following linking words:

word bank   because   and   also

Here is what you need to do:

- Begin by dating the letter and addressing the teacher.
- Then, write your opinion and reasons.
- Finally, sign your letter.

You can use the template below.

Date: _____

Dear Mr./Mrs. Teacher,

   I believe the class should get _____

(your opinion) **because** (list your reasons) _____

_____

_____

_____

_____

_____

             Sincerely, _____

Special People in American History

In this unit you will explore the lives of two people with amazing qualities. You will learn from their experiences and will appreciate how their actions have shaped our country for the better.

Sequoyah's Gift

1   One man accomplished in just twelve short years what could have taken hundreds of years for someone else. In 1821, a Native American man named Sequoyah (S-si-qua-ya) invented the Cherokee **syllabary**. This written code of symbols connects to sounds that make up the Cherokee language. This was a special gift that has allowed Cherokee people to read and write in their own language.

2   Sequoyah spoke many different languages. While in the army, he became **inspired** by other soldiers. He watched them write markings on paper to **communicate**. They wrote letters home to their families; they could read army orders. As a result, Sequoyah decided to create a written language for the Cherokee people. He began to study different ways the language could be written.

3   In 1809, Sequoyah began to focus on creating symbols for each syllable spoken in the Cherokee language. After working for a total of twelve years, he invented a Cherokee writing system using true phonetic symbols. It was a written language made up of eighty-six symbols: consonant-vowel combinations, six vowels, and the consonant s. In 1821, Sequoyah introduced his writing system to the Cherokee Nation.

4   Thousands of the Cherokee learned to read and write! Use of the writing system led the way for the first Cherokee newspaper. Books such as the Bible as well as some educational materials became available in Cherokee.

5   Today, Sequoyah's syllabary is important to the educational programs of the Cherokee Nations in Oklahoma and North Carolina. His memory is **honored** at **Sequoia National Park** in California, where two types of giant redwood trees are named after him.

glossary

Communicate: To share information

Honored: To give respect

Inspired: To cause a person to have feelings to take action

Translated: To change words from one language to another

Syllabary: A set of written characters that represent different syllables

Ready, Set, Climb!

For an exciting video experience, visit the website below and join scientists as they climb and study the largest tree in the world, "The President," at Sequoia National Park!

Digging Deeper

ngm.nationalgeographic.com/2012/12/sequoias/behind-the-scenes-video

AUTHOR'S PURPOSE

Use "Sequoyah's Gift" to answer the following questions.

Why did the author write this passage?

    A. To describe the importance of language

    B. To show that Sequoyah was a very smart person

    C. To explain how the Cherokee written language came to be

PICTURES HELP EXPLAIN A TEXT

Look at the pictures of the giant trees in Sequoia National Park. Answer the following question.

Why was naming two types of Redwood trees after Sequoyah a good thing to do?

    A. Sequoyah lived in a part of the country where these trees are found.

    B. The trees have been a part of America's history almost as long as Native Americans have lived in America.

    C. There are no other trees like these in America and there has never been a person in America to create a written language like Sequoyah.

COMPARING FORMAL AND INFORMAL LANGUAGE

When speaking or writing we use either **informal** or **formal** language. We use informal language when we write or speak to our friends.

Types of informal writing:

- Text messages and personal emails
- Short notes
- Friendly letters
- Blogs
- Diaries

Example: **Shucks!** The Indian Museum is closed for the season.

There are not as many rules for informal writing because we are writing to family and friends.

However, we would not speak or talk to the school principal the same way as we would to our friends or family. When talking or writing to the principal, we would use formal language.

Types of formal writing:

- Business letters
- Letters of complaint
- Some essays
- Reports
- Official speeches
- Announcements
- Professional emails

In formal writing, we:

- do not use contractions (for example, haven't, wasn't)

- spell out numbers less than 100 (for example, seven instead of 7)

- write in third person point of view (avoiding words like *I* and *me*)

- do not use slang words and phrases (such as "What's up?")

Example: The Indian Museum is closed for the season.

Activity 1

Write an "I" beside the sentences that you would include in an informal letter and an "F" beside the sentences that you would include in a formal letter.

1. _____ Sequoyah was a smart dude to create the Cherokee alphabet.

2. _____ We appreciate that you chose our school to visit this year.

3. _____ We're happy that you decided to visit our awesome town.

4. _____ I think it's cool that you're going to teach us the Cherokee language!

5. _____ It took Sequoyah almost twelve years to create the Cherokee syllabary.

Activity 2

Circle the informal writing used in the formal letter below. Explain how you would make it formal in the space below.

456 Little Street
Cojack MO 00987
August 8, 2014

Dear Principal Chawla,

We're so lucky we have a great principal like you! Our teacher told us that you lived on an Indian reservation for 15 years. Dude, that is so cool! We wanted to ask you a favor. Can you please arrange a time to tell us about your life on the reservation? We would also love to see photos if you have any available.

Thank you,
Mrs. Barron's class

_____

_____

_____

_____

USING GLOSSARIES AND DICTIONARIES

Glossaries and dictionaries explain what words mean. Glossaries are sometimes located at the backs of books or ends of articles. Dictionaries have **guide words** at the tops of the pages to help you locate where the word you are trying to find appears in the dictionary.

Activity 1

Use the glossary at the end of the article to answer the questions below.

1. When you **honor** your parents you are giving them this. _____

2. You can do this by sending an email to your friend. _____

3. If you **translate** something, what are you doing? _____

Activity 2

Read the dictionary guide words on each feather. Then read the words in the word bank below. Write each word on the feather that has the correct guide word you would need for finding the word in a dictionary.

word bank   Alphabet   Cherokee   Indian   Symbol

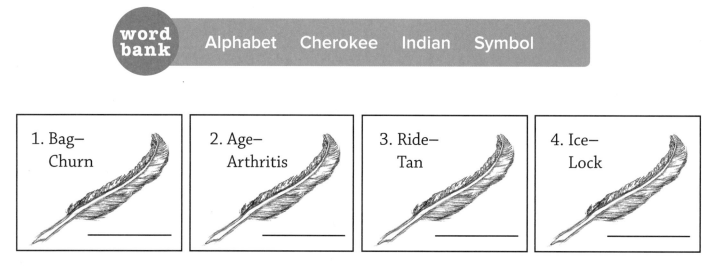

1. Bag–
   Churn
   _____

2. Age–
   Arthritis
   _____

3. Ride–
   Tan
   _____

4. Ice–
   Lock
   _____

Challenge: Pretend you are writing a formal letter to a very important Native American leader. Make sure to follow the rules for formal writing. Include a few words from the glossary in your letter, and use a dictionary.

Ride!

1 Have you ever dreamed of being an astronaut? Sally Ride never thought it would be possible. But in 1977, Ride saw an ad in her college newspaper asking people who wanted to become astronauts to apply to NASA. She was so excited to find out that they were looking for women to join the team!

NASA

2 When Ride entered **NASA** in 1978, she had to complete very hard training. Ride had to learn special skills like parachute jumping, water safety, and map reading. She also worked on skills for flying in space like moving in **weightlessness** and using radio **communication**. Ride enjoyed flight training so much that she decided to take up flying as a **hobby**!

Into Space and Beyond

3 On June 13, 1983, one of Ride's dreams came true. She was the first American woman to fly to outer space! She took off on the Challenger space shuttle from the Kennedy Space Center in Florida. Sally and the flight crew of the Challenger were in flight for 147 hours! After that trip, Sally flew one more flight to space before going to work on a special team for the president. She spent the rest of her life working to help others love math and science as much as she did. Sally also co-wrote many science books for children. In 2001, she started a company called Sally Ride Science to **encourage** young people (especially girls) to take more science and math classes in school.

Awards

4 While Ride was alive she was given many honors and awards. She was even chosen to be in the **Astronaut Hall of Fame**! After her death in 2012, she was given the highest medal any person can get in the United States: the Presidential Medal of Freedom. Ride was a very special American who spent much of her life **devoted** to NASA. She worked hard to share her hopes, dreams, and love of space with people.

glossary

Astronaut Hall of Fame: A museum that features the world's largest collection of personal astronaut collectables

Communication: An exchange of information

Devoted: Having strong love for something or someone

Encourage: To make someone hopeful

Hobby: An activity someone does for fun

NASA: Short for the National Aeronautics and Space Administration, a U.S. government organization responsible for space travel and research

Weightlessness: Having little weight

Make Your Own Space Shuttle!

Using a few household items, you can make your very own model of a space shuttle. Visit the website below and have some fun!

Digging Deeper

www.bry-backmanor.org/space/shuttlecraft.html

USING TEXT FEATURES

Use "Ride!" to answer the following questions.

1. Under which subheading can you find information about Ride's flight training?

    A. NASA

    B. Awards

    C. Into Space and Beyond

2. Under which subheading can you find information about the medal Ride received after her death?

    A. NASA

    B. Awards

    C. Into Space and Beyond

3. What is the box at the end of the article called?

    A. caption

    B. glossary

    C. hyperlink

Bold words located within the text are called **subheadings**. These tell you what information that section contains. **Captions** are short definitions that explain pictures.

Standard RI.2.5

AUTHOR'S PURPOSE

Use "Ride!" to answer the following questions.

1. Why did the author write this article?

   A. To describe NASA

   B. To describe how hard it is to become an astronaut

   C. To describe the first American woman who went into space

2. What information in the section **Into Space and Beyond** supports this statement from the conclusion of the article?

   "She worked hard to share her hopes, dreams, and love of space with people."

   _____

   _____

   _____

   _____

3. In the beginning of the article, the author writes about Ride seeing a newspaper ad for NASA. What information in the article tells you that she not only applied for but also got into NASA?

   _____

   _____

   _____

   _____

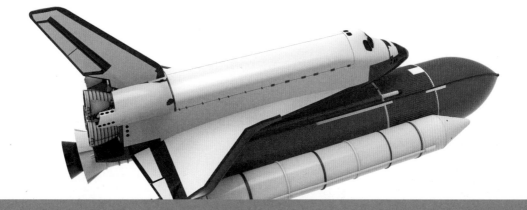

USING REFERENCE MATERIAL

A glossary or dictionary is a type of reference material that lists words in alphabetical order with the definitions of the words. It is also used to locate correct spelling, meaning, and grammar usage for words.

Look at the dictionary items below. After reading the words and definitions, answer the questions the follow.

Survival
1. The act of living; the state or fact of continuing to live or exist especially in spite of difficult conditions

Navigation
1. The act of finding a way to get to a place while on a ship, aircraft, boat, etc., ...

Weightlessness
1. Being without weight, a body acted upon by a force that neutralizes gravity

Communication
1. The act or process of using words, sounds, signs, or behaviors to express or exchange information or to express your ideas, thoughts, feelings, etc., to someone else

2. Imparting or interchanging thoughts, opinions, or information by speech, writing, or signs

1. Directing the course for a spaceship is called what?

    A. navigashion

    B. navigation

    C. navgtion

2. What is it called when someone or something continues to exist when conditions are difficult?

    A. servival

    B. survivel

    C. survival

COLLECTIVE NOUNS

A noun is a person, place, or thing. When a noun refers to a group of people it is called a **collective noun**.

Circle the collective noun in each sentence below.

1. Sally and the flight crew were in space for 147 hours.

2. Sally Ride's family accepted the awards for her after her death in 2012.

3. Sally Ride Science is a company formed to help kids continue to learn math and science.

ADJECTIVES

Writers use descriptive words to help readers understand the information better. **Adjectives** describe nouns. Writers use adjectives to describe the qualities of people, things and places.

Read the sentences below. Fill in each blank with an adjective from the word bank that makes the sentence more descriptive.

word bank   heavy   bright   difficult

1. In space, there are many _____ stars to see.

2. The training for astronauts is very _____.

3. Astronauts wear _____ space suits.

WRITE YOUR ESSAY

Imagine you are training to become an astronaut. You have just been selected for the moon space program. You are excited. But you also know it is not an easy trip to make. Write about the good things and the not so good things about going to the moon. With the help of an adult, do a little research on the subject online or at your local library. Use the organizer below to plan your essay.

Going to the Moon

Good	Not So Good
Fact _____ _____	Fact _____ _____
Supporting Reason _____ _____	Supporting Reason _____ _____
Fact _____ _____	Fact _____ _____
Supporting Reason _____ _____	Supporting Reason _____ _____

WRITE YOUR ESSAY

Use your outline from page 82 to develop your essay below. Plan an introduction, a body, and a conclusion.

Introduction:

_____

_____

_____

_____

_____

_____

Body:

_____

_____

_____

_____

_____

_____

Conclusion:

_____

_____

_____

_____

_____

_____

Historical Landmarks of America

The United States of America has many geographic and historical landmarks! Are you ready for a mini-trip around the country? In this unit, you will travel to fun locations and learn of their special place in American history.

Enjoy your reading journey!

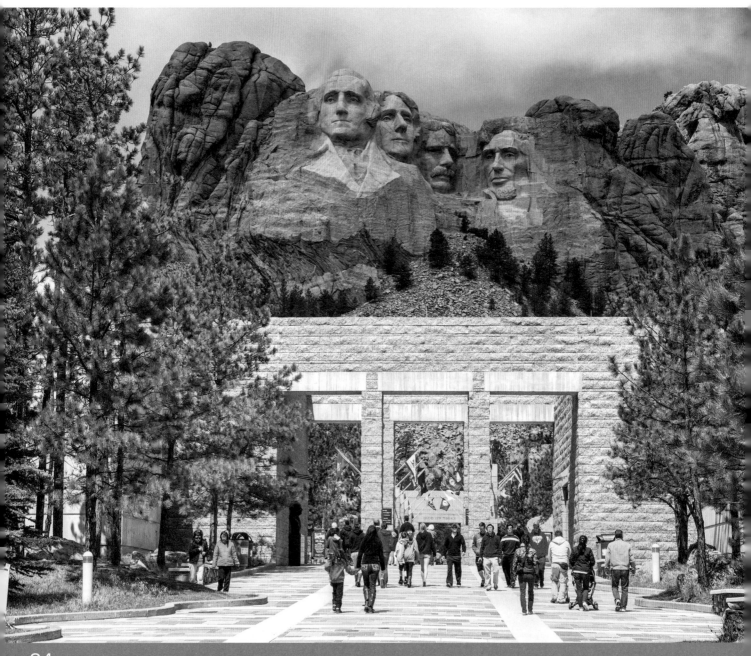

Mt. Rushmore

| About | Who Are We | Cool Books | Contact Us |

A Grand Idea

South Dakota is a wonderful place to live! However, a long time ago, South Dakota had a difficult time attracting visitors. The state historian, Doane Robinson, contacted a sculptor by the name of Gutzon Borglum and told him of a great idea!

In order to bring people to South Dakota, Robinson imagined that the Black Hills of South Dakota would have large figures carved into the sides of one of the mountains. The work was started on October 4, 1927, and it took 14 long years to complete!

The Faces of Mt. Rushmore

Borglum loved the idea, but wanted to choose four important faces to place on the mountain. He chose four presidents: George Washington, Abraham Lincoln, Thomas Jefferson, and Theodore Roosevelt. These faces were important because they represented the first 150 years of American history.

About	Who Are We	Cool Books	Contact Us

My Favorite Facts

Here are some cool facts about Mt. Rushmore that visitors may want to know:

- Mt. Rushmore is 5,725 feet tall

- Mt. Rushmore was named in 1885 for a New York lawyer named Charles E. Rushmore

- Average snowfall is about 10–20 inches per year

- If you visit Mt. Rushmore, you are likely to see a number of animals including bison, elk, sheep, and bobcats.

Rocky Mountain Goat
Oreamnos americanus

Mule Deer
Odocoileus hemionus

Mt. Rushmore is now visited by millions of people each year! For more information, please visit: *www.nps.gov/Mt.Rushmore*

UNDERSTANDING TEXT FEATURES

Text features help the reader to locate and understand information. There are many different types of text features, but here are a few common ones:

Key Words	Highlighted or bolded words in a text	A visitor to a historic landmark is called a **tourist**.
Hyperlinks	Electronic connector that allows readers to move from one document to another	*www.nps.gov/Mt.Rushmore*
Subheadings	A heading that includes a section of information related to that topic	**Types of Landmarks** • shipwrecks • battlefields • homes • tombs
Glossary	Gives the meaning of words	**Habitat**: place where plant or animal naturally lives
Caption	Gives information about a picture	Rocky Mountain Goat *Oreamnos americanus*
Tabs	Tell us where to find information	**Who Are We**
Icon	A sign or symbol that represents its meaning by how it looks	

Activity 1

Answer the following questions about text features.

1. Which type of text feature does the author include to help the reader learn more about the picture?

    A. glossary   B. caption   C. hyperlink

2. Which subheading includes information about how Mt. Rushmore began?

    A. The Grand Idea   B. My Favorite Facts   C. The Faces of Mt. Rushmore

3. What is this icon a picture of?

    A. lollipop   B. glasses   C. magnifying glass

4. If you click the above icon, what will you be able to do?

    A. search for information   B. go to the home page   C. exit the page

5. Which of the following tabs would you use to locate different books to read about Mt. Rushmore?

    A. About Us   B. Cool Books   C. Contact Us

6. Which of the following tabs would you use to email a question to someone who works for the national memorial?

    A. About Us   B. Cool Books   C. Contact Us

Activity 2

Look at the text feature on the left. In the box to the right, write what kind of text feature it is.

Text Feature	Name of Feature
Least Chipmunk *Tamias minimus*	
A Grand Idea	
For more information, please visit: *www.nps.gov/Mt.Rushmore*	

IRREGULAR PLURAL NOUNS

Most nouns can be made plural by adding an **s** or **es** to the end of the word. However, some nouns do not follow the rules. They are called irregular nouns. Irregular nouns do not become plural by adding **s** or **es** but rather by changing the spelling of the word or changing the last letter of the word before adding **s**. For instance, the word **loaf** becomes *loaves* by changing the **f** to **ve** and adding an **s**. Another example is the plural form of **man**, which is *men*.

Complete the chart below. The first column has a picture of the singular version of the noun. Please write the word below the picture. In the second column, write its plural version. Then, write a sentence using the plural noun in the third column.

Singular	Plural	Plural used in a sentence
1. _____		
2. _____		
3. _____		

USING COMMAS IN GREETINGS AND CLOSINGS OF LETTERS

When writing a letter it is important to make sure to place **commas** in the correct places. Commas should always be placed in the greetings, closings, and dates of letters.

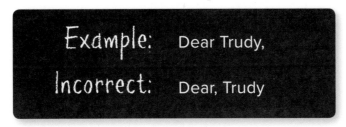

Example: Dear Trudy,

Incorrect: Dear, Trudy

Underline the correct way to write greetings, dates, and closings in letters.

1. Which greeting is written correctly?

    A. Dear Elise,

    B. Dear, Elise

    C. Dear Elise

2. Which closing is written correctly?

    A. Your friend

    B. Your friend!

    C. Your friend,

3. Which date from the text is written correctly?

    A. October 4, 1925

    B. July 4, 1930,

    C. August, 30, 1936

Activity 2

Read the letter. Circle all of the commas that you find. Then, answer the questions that follow.

1. In the greeting, the comma should go after

   A. Chidi

   B. aunt

   C. Dear

2. In the closing, the comma should go after

   A. love

   B. your

   C. nephew

Dear Aunt Chidi   March 21, 2015

We are having a wonderful time in South Dakota. Today, we went to Mt. Rushmore! Mom, Dad, Hayden, and I had so much fun. We saw a lot of wild animals and met some very nice people. We took lots of pictures with our phones. I emailed some to you already. Aunt Chidi, you will have to come with us the next time.

I can't wait to see you when we get back home.

Love
Your nephew Andreas

Challenge: Imagine that you have been asked to suggest that another face be added into Mt. Rushmore. Write a letter to a friend explaining which historical American figure deserves to have his or her face on Mt. Rushmore. Make sure to place the commas in the correct places, and use at least two irregular plural nouns in your letter.

_____

_____

_____

_____

_____

_____

_____

_____

_____

_____

REVIEW

Congratulations! You have completed the lessons in this section. Now you will have the opportunity to practice some of the skills you just learned.

Reading Fluency

Adults: Time your student for one minute while he or she is reading to you. Make a note of where he or she is after one minute to track your student's fluency. (Your student should be able to read 60–90 words per minute). Then, have your student continue reading to the end of the article and answer the questions that follow.

A Famous Masterpiece

1 Have you ever built a masterpiece? Something so amazing that there is not anything else 15
like it? A man named William F. Lamb did. He helped design a building so tall that for forty 34
years it was the tallest building in America. It was even in a popular movie, *King Kong*. Today, 52
it is of one of the most famous buildings in the world. What building is it? It's the Empire 71
State Building! 73

2 Impossible to miss, this famous skyscraper stands over 1,250 feet high. Each year 86
millions of people visit New York to see the amazing views from the 102nd floor. But 102
watch out! This building is topped with a lightning rod. It is struck by lightning around 118
100 times a year! 122

3 Lamb created the design for the building in just two short weeks. A little over a 138
year later, on May 1, 1931, the Empire State Building opened. Since then, the building 153
has become famous for its style. More than 161
3,000 workers were needed to build it. The 169
workers used around 57,000 tons of steel, 176
2 million cubic feet of stone, and 10 million 185
bricks to complete the job. The building 192
weighs a whopping 365,000 tons! 197

4 Each year a race up the stairs to the 206
86th floor is held. Runners must climb a total of 216
1,576 steps! Even though it is no longer America's 225
tallest building, the Empire State Building is a symbol of 235
hope. People can work together to reach amazing **goals**! 244

Words read in 1 minute – errors = WPM

Standard RF.3.4.b

Activity 1

Underline the informal sentence. Circle the formal sentence.

1. Wouldn't it be awesome to visit the Empire State Building?

2. We are looking forward to our field trip to the Empire State Building in three days.

Activity 2

Use a dictionary to create a glossary for the words below.

1. Goal _____

2. Style _____

3. Masterpiece _____

4. Design _____

Activity 3

Choose the correct collective noun from the box for each word. *Hint:* **Two collective nouns do not belong.**

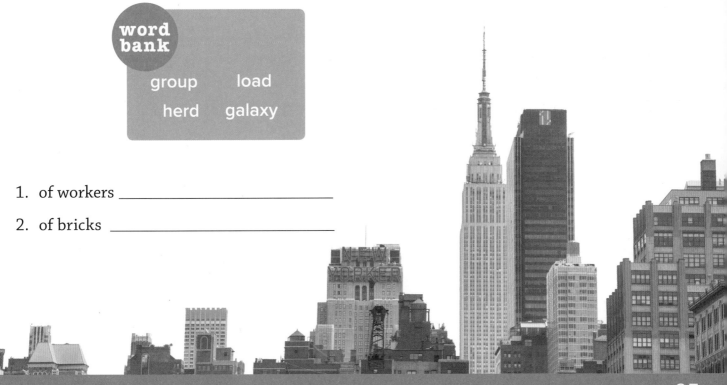

word bank

group   load
herd   galaxy

1. of workers _____

2. of bricks _____

Activity 4

Fill in each blank with an adjective of your choice.

1. The Empire State Building is a(an) _____ building and _____ landmark.

2. People can see the _____ views from the _____ windows of the 102nd floor.

Activity 5

Look at the dictionary words to answer the questions below.

> **skyscraper** (noun)
>   1. A very tall building with many stories
>
> **architecture** (noun)
>   1. The art or science of designing and building
>
> **amazing** (adjective)
>   1. Causing great surprise or wonder

1. Which word is not a noun? _____

2. Write the definition of the word **skyscraper**. _____

_____

Activity 6

Write the plural form of each irregular noun.

Person _____

Life _____

Activity 7

Circle the correctly punctuated greeting or closing.

1.   Dear, Mr. Lamb   Dear Mr. Lamb,   Dear Mr., Lamb

2.   Your buddy,   Your, buddy   Your, buddy,

Activity 8

Rewrite the misspelled words correctly.

scaired _____

graype _____

Activity 9

Look back at how the word *goal* is used in the article. Use what you learned about identifying connections between words in a text and words in real life to name two goals that you would like to achieve.

1. _____

2. _____

Ellen Ochoa

1 Have you ever been asked what you want to be when you grow up? If you haven't figured it out yet, you're not alone. The important thing is to set a **goal** and work towards reaching it. Ellen Ochoa did just that. She became the first Hispanic woman astronaut in the world.

Ochoa's Childhood

2 Ellen Ochoa was born in southern California in 1958. In school, she loved math and science. She also enjoyed playing the flute. She wanted to be a musician when she grew up.

Following Dreams

3 When Ochoa was in high school, some of the students put her down because she liked science. Even a few teachers did not believe she would ever do well in science. Luckily, she did not listen to those people. She decided to keep studying science.

Sally Ride—An Example to Follow

4 In the 1970s while Ochoa was in college studying physics, **NASA** hired its first woman astronaut, Sally Ride. This event, along with Ochoa's interest in engineering and space exploration research, **encouraged** her to apply for the astronaut program once she received her college degree.

Ochoa Never Quits

5 The first time Ochoa applied to NASA, they did not accept her. But she did not give up hope. Five years later, in 1991, she applied again. This time, she got the job! She worked hard. In 1993, she went into space for the first time aboard the shuttle Discovery. She had to **deploy**

and capture a research satellite to study the sun. That mission lasted ninety days. In 1994, she boarded the shuttle Atlantis, where she was a payload commander for Mission STS-66. She also flew in 1999, and again in 2002. To date, Ochoa has spent 719 hours in space and has flown millions of miles!

Additional Accomplishments

Besides being an astronaut, Ochoa is also an inventor. She has invented robots, **optical recognition** systems, and computer **hardware**. Her inventions help NASA to sharpen and improve images from space. One of her greatest **accomplishments** is being a mother to her son, whom she stays in contact with through video chats in space. She also talks to young girls and encourages them to follow their dreams. She believes the keys to success are teamwork and to never stop learning.

Ellen Ochoa never let what the others said stop her from reaching her goals. As a result, when she grew up she became a mother, an inventor, and the first Hispanic woman to ever go into space.

glossary

Accomplishments: A result, skill or ability received through hard work and special efforts

Deploy: To organize and send people out for a particular purpose

Goal: The object toward which effort is directed

Hardware: Equipment used for a particular purpose

Inspire: To cause someone to take action

NASA: American government space agency, National Aeronautics and Space Administration

Optical recognition: Technology that recognizes, scans, and reads text and images

Use "Ellen Ochoa" to answer the following questions.

1. Which award did Ellen Ochoa earn first?

   _____

Award	Year
NASA's Exceptional Service Medal	1997
Outstanding Leadership Medal	1995
Space Flight Medals	2002, 1999 1994, 1993

2. Which award did Ochoa earn in 1995?

   _____

3. How many times did Ellen earn the Space Flight Medal?

   _____

4. Read the following sentence.

   She tells the girls to look to teachers for help in following their dreams.

   Under which subheading would this sentence appear if it were included in the article?

   _____

5. Under which subheading would the reader find where Ochoa was born?

   _____

6. Why did the author write this article?

   A. To convince the reader to become an astronaut

   B. To prove that Ochoa is the best astronaut in the world

   C. To inform the reader about Ellen Ochoa, the first Hispanic woman astronaut

7. The author says that people should set goals and work toward them. What reason(s) does the author give in the text?

   _____

8. The author says Ellen Ochoa was encouraged to become an astronaut. What reason(s) does the author give to support this?

_____

9. Reread the following sentence from the article.

   *"In 1994, she **boarded** the shuttle Atlantis, where she was a payload commander for Mission STS-66."*

   What is the meaning of the word **boarded** as in the sentence above?

   A. flew

   B. entered

   C. left

10. Reread the following sentence from the article.

   *"Her inventions help NASA to **sharpen** and improve images from space."*

   Which sentence best uses the word **sharpen** in the same way as in the sentence above?

   A. The boy went to the front of the class to sharpen his pencil.

   B. Calvin's teacher says he must sharpen his math skills.

   C. The photographer will sharpen the picture to make it clearer.

What would you say? Let's take what you have learned and write about it!

Write Your Essay

Do you know what you would like to be when you grow up? Do you have a special dream that you want to follow?

Write an essay about what you would like to be when you grow up. Describe what you will do to follow your dreams. Use the graphic organizer on page 103 to write a strong introduction and descriptive details that support your ideas. List a series of events that you feel will help you reach your goals. Do a little research on your topic with the help of an adult. Finally, write a conclusion that sums up your plan of action.

Topic: What do you want to be when you grow up?

_____

_____

_____

_____

Standard W.2.3

Introduction (Clearly state your dreams and goals):

_____

_____

_____

Step 1 (What can you do to reach your goal? Provide evidence and facts to support your plan of action):

_____

_____

_____

Step 2 (Provide evidence and facts to support your plan of action):

_____

_____

_____

Step 3 (Provide evidence and facts to support your plan of action):

_____

_____

_____

Conclusion (Restate your dream and what you will do to reach it):

_____

_____

_____

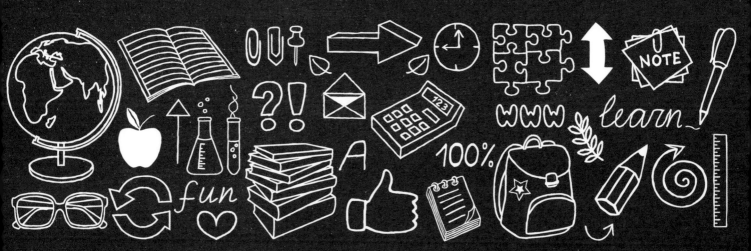

Reading and Writing: Literature

Diversity in Cultures

In this section, you will read stories, myths, and poems with amazing plots, interesting characters, and beautiful word pictures.

Reading literature provides a look into an author's thoughts and feelings. It also reflects our world and the different ways that people behave. Even though the material in this section is fictional, valuable life lessons can be learned. Reading literature can affect how you think and feel, which in turn can shape your actions.

Writing about literature will cause you to organize your thoughts so that you will be able to clearly state your point of view. As you write, new discoveries in your thinking will create connections to ideas and concepts that you already know. Working through what at first may seem challenging will open new pathways of learning, understanding, and communicating.

While reading literature teaches you how other people behave, writing about literature teaches you about yourself!

Happy reading and writing!

WHAT IS CULTURE?

Culture is a set of beliefs, ideas, and ways of doing things that is shared by a group of people. The people in the group must have something in common. It could be the place they live now, where their ancestors lived, or their religion. Everyone belongs to a culture, and some people belong to more than one!

Learning about different cultures helps people understand each other and get along better. One way to learn about another culture is to read stories from that culture. The characters in a culture's stories speak, think, and act like people from their culture. If the story tells a lesson, it is probably a lesson that is important to that culture.

The first story in this unit, "The King Who Caught a Thief," is a folktale from the country of India. Folktales are stories that are passed down from parents to their children, and then again to the children's children, and so on. They usually have a moral, or lesson, that they teach. As you read, think about what the story can teach you about Indian culture.

The King Who Caught a Thief

Long ago in India, a man pretended to be a very poor **Brahmin**. He sat in the middle of his town with a basket. People put money in his basket because they thought helping him would make the gods happy. In return, he gave them good **advice**. He got very **famous** for his advice. Soon he had a lot of money.

The man could have helped other poor people with his money, but instead he kept it for himself. Every day he went out to the forest and buried it under a tree. Then he went back to town with his basket empty. He wore his oldest clothes and tried to look as poor as possible, so people would keep giving him money.

One day when he went out to count his money, it was gone! The man went back into the town very angry. He was so upset about the **theft** that he told the people in the town everything.

"I am not really poor," he said. "I have been keeping all the money for myself. Now someone has stolen it! I must get my money back!"

"What you did was very wrong," the people said. "You lied to us and pretended to be poor."

That made him even angrier. He did not want people to tell him he was wrong. He wanted help getting his money back!

"If you do not help me, I will go away to the **Ganges River**, and never come back!" he said. The people were upset he had lied to them, but they did not want him to leave. They liked his good advice. So they took him to the king of the town. He told the king his whole story.

"Even though you are very greedy," the king said, "I will help you get your money back. I promise." The king kept his promise and caught the thief. The thief was very sorry for what he had done. He promised to never steal again, so the king let him go.

The king gave the money back to the man. However, the man was still not happy. "You must punish the thief!" he said to the king. "I will not leave the palace until you do!" But the

glossary

Brahmin: A priest, or holy man, in the Hindu religion, one of the religions in India

Advice: Ideas or help you might give to someone who has a problem or is having trouble making a decision

Famous: Well known to many people

Theft: The act of stealing, or taking something that belongs to someone else

without their permission. Someone who steals is called a thief.

Ganges River: A river in India that is sacred, or holy, in the Hindu religion

Palace: A large, fine house where a ruler, such as a king, lives

Servant: Someone whose job is to serve, or do things for, another person

king was tired of helping the greedy man. He asked two of his **servants** to take the money outside the palace. The man had to follow them out of the palace, pick up his money, and leave. No one knows what happened to the man after that day.

CENTRAL THEME AND CHARACTERS

Use "The King Who Caught a Thief" to answer the following questions.

1. How did the people respond when the man told them he was not really poor?

    A. They took the man to the king.

    B. They helped the man catch the thief.

    C. They ordered the man to leave.

2. How did the man act when the king returned his money to him?

    _____

    _____

    _____

3. What does that tell you about the man?

    _____

    _____

    _____

4. How does the king respond when the man orders him to punish the thief?

    _____

    _____

5. What is the main idea of this story, or the lesson that it is trying to teach? (*Hint:* You may find it helpful to look back over the story and your answers to the other questions!)

    _____

    _____

LOOKING AT STORY STRUCTURE

When you are building a house with blocks (or even in real life), do you start with the roof? Of course not! Usually, the roof is the last thing you put on a house. First, you have to build something that can hold the roof up, like walls. And before you build the walls, you need a floor, or foundation, to build on. Just like a block house has to be built from the bottom up, a story needs to be built in a certain order.

Use "The King Who Caught a Thief" to answer the following questions.

1. What happens at the beginning of the story?

   A. A man pretends to be poor and people give him money for advice.

   B. A man goes to get his money and discovers that a thief has stolen it.

   C. A man threatens to leave the town if the people do not help him.

2. What happens at the end of the story?

   A. The king promises the man he will return his money.

   B. The man picks up his money and leaves the palace.

   C. The people take the man to the king's palace.

3. What is the man's point of view about the stolen money?

   A. The money was never really his, but he would like it back anyway.

   B. The money is his and everyone should help him get it back.

   C. The money belongs to the gods so he must find it because he is a holy man.

4. How does the king feel about the man? Use details from the story in your answer.

   _____

   _____

   _____

   _____

   _____

MAKING CONNECTIONS WITH PICTURES

Use "The King Who Caught a Thief" to answer the questions below.

1. Which character is in the illustration on page 109?

   _____

   _____

2. How do you know?

   _____

   _____

LEARNING ABOUT LANGUAGE

Nouns are words for people, places, and things. **Pronouns** are words that can replace one or more nouns. Consider this example:

Example: "**Amanda** bought the **puppy** for **Mitchell**."

"Amanda," "puppy," and "Mitchell" are all **nouns**. If you were having a conversation with your friend, you could just keep using the **nouns** "Amanda," "puppy," and "Mitchell" over and over again, like this:

Example:
You: "**Amanda** bought the **puppy** for **Mitchell**."
Your friend: "When did **Amanda** buy the **puppy** for **Mitchell**?"
You: "**Amanda** bought the **puppy** on Friday."

But you would probably get tired of repeating them pretty quickly! Now, take a look at the conversation with **pronouns**:

Example:
You: "Amanda bought the puppy for Mitchell."
Your friend: "When did **she** buy **it** for **him**?"
You: "**She** bought **it** on Friday."

"She" replaced "Amanda," "it" replaced "the puppy," and "he" replaced "Mitchell." But what if Mitchell was the one who bought the puppy?

Consider the example:

Example: "**Mitchell** bought the **puppy** for **Mitchell**."

Unless there are two people named Mitchell, this sentence would sound odd. However, a regular **pronoun** does not work here, as this example shows:

Example: "**He** bought **it** for **him**."

"Him" could be anyone! How can it be changed to identify that "he" and "him" are the same person—Mitchell? You need a special pronoun called **a reflexive pronoun**! Reflexive pronouns are usually made by adding "-self" to a form of the pronoun, like this:

Example: "**He** bought **it** for **himself**."

Use "The King Who Caught a Thief" to answer the following questions.

1. Look at the sentence from the story:

   "The man could have helped other poor people with his money, but instead he kept it for himself."

   A. What reflexive pronoun is used in the sentence?

   _____

   B. What noun is it replacing?

   _____

2. Look back at the story carefully. What other reflexive pronoun can you find? Write the sentence in the space below, and circle the reflexive pronoun in the sentence.

   _____

   _____

   _____

USING CAPITAL LETTERS

Some nouns, called proper nouns, always start with a capital letter. Place names can be proper nouns—but only if the place is unique, or the only place like it on Earth. For example, a park is a type of place, but you would not use a capital letter to say, "I am going to the park." If you name a specific, unique park, though, a capital letter would be used; for example, "I am going to Central Park." Central and Park have capital letters because they are the name of a unique place, Central Park, in New York City, New York.

1. Which word is a proper noun that should start with a capital letter?

   A. India

   B. Town

   C. Palace

2. Look back at the story. Can you find another name of a place that is also a proper noun? Write it in the space below.

   _____

   _____

   _____

Digging Deeper

Expand Your Knowledge: Reflexive Pronouns

There are more reflexive pronouns that are not used in this story. Do you know any of them? With the help of a parent or other responsible adult, visit the websites listed below. The first website tells you about different reflexive pronouns and gives examples of how to use them. The second website has a quick quiz where you can test your learning!

www.grammar-monster.com/glossary/reflexive_pronouns.htm

www.softschools.com/quizzes/grammar/reflexive_pronouns/quiz429.html

WRITE YOUR NARRATIVE

No one knows what happened after the man picked up his money and left the palace—except for you! Imagine that you are the only person from the town who knows what happened to the man. Write "Part Two" of the story, using the space below. Make sure you use complete sentences, and check your story for correct spelling and punctuation when you are finished! The first sentence is already written to help you get started.

No one knew what happened to the man after that day except for me.

_____

_____

_____

_____

_____

_____

_____

_____

_____

_____

_____

_____

_____

_____

_____

Some stories are told just for fun. Other stories teach lessons. One type of story that teaches a lesson is called a fable. Fables are usually very short stories. They have characters that are animals, but the animals talk and act like people. The moral, or lesson that the fable is teaching, is usually at the end. Sometimes one of the characters says the moral. Other times the moral is a sentence that follows the story.

The most famous fable writer was Aesop. He lived hundreds of years ago. His fables are still read and enjoyed because of the good lessons they teach.

"No act of kindness, no matter how small, is ever wasted."
– Aesop

The Lion and the Boar

One hot summer day, a thirsty lion and boar came to a small pool of water. They began to argue over who should drink first. So the lion roared and said, "I am king of the jungle, so I will take the first drink!" "Oh, no!" the boar grunted loudly, "My tusks can tear an animal to shreds, so I will take the first drink." The lion growled at the boar. Then the boar, with stiff legs and hair standing on end, pushed the lion. In a rage, the lion smacked the boar with his mighty paw. So the lion and the boar battled long and hard—almost to the death. The two creatures felt very tired. They paused to catch their breath. Just then, they saw a vulture in a tree above them. The vulture was waiting to feast on the animal that lost the battle. Now

both animals understood that a dead animal is food for a vulture. Thinking about this, the lion said, "The vulture saw us fighting. If one of us kills the other, the vulture will be happy." "You are right!" said the boar. "Go ahead and drink from the well first." "No, my friend you drink first," said the lion. So the lion and the boar took turns drinking from the pool. They decided that it was better to be friends than to become food for a hungry vulture.

CENTRAL MESSAGE AND CHARACTERS

We can figure out the **central message** or lesson—often called the "moral of the story"—through key details in the text.

Use "The Lion and the Boar" to answer the following questions.

1. What is the **moral** of the story?

   A. Good things come to those who wait

   B. Don't count your chickens before they hatch

   C. Watch out for those who will benefit from your loss

2 Which sentence helps you find the **moral**, or lesson of the story?

   A. "They began to argue over who should drink first."

   B. "So the lion and the boar battled long and hard—almost to the death."

   C. "They decided that it was better to be friends, than to become food for a hungry vulture."

3. What problem do the lion and the boar have at the end of the story?

   _____

   _____

   _____

   _____

   _____

4. How do the lion and the boar deal with the problem?

   _____

   _____

   _____

   _____

   _____

PARTS OF A STORY

Connecting the beginning, middle, and end of a story helps you to understand it better.

Use "The Lion and the Boar" to answer the following questions.

1. How might the story have changed if the lion and boar had not become friends?

   _____

   _____

   _____

   _____

2. What is the lion's opinion of the vulture?

   A. He thinks the vulture is evil.

   B. He thinks the vulture is clever.

   C. He thinks the vulture is foolish.

3. Would the moral change if the vulture were not in the story?

   _____

   _____

   _____

   _____

4. How does the boar feel about the lion at the end of the story?

   A. He likes him.

   B. He looks up to him.

   C. He is proud of him.

SIMPLE AND COMPOUND SENTENCES

There are many different types of sentences. These include simple and compound.

A **simple sentence** is a sentence with only one subject and predicate and one complete thought.

Example: The boar is wild.

A **compound sentence** is a sentence with two or more complete thoughts that are joined by a comma and words that connect the sentence parts (a conjunction) such as *for, and, not, but,* and *so*.

Example: I want to pet the boar, but it is a wild animal.

Activity 1

Decide whether each sentence is a simple or compound sentence. Circle the letter in the matching column. Then, solve the riddle on the next page!

Sentences	Simple	Compound
1. A lion was thirsty.	H	B
2. The lion wanted a drink, but the boar would not let him.	C	E
3. The boar pushed the lion, and the lion smacked the boar.	W	T
4. The lion was very angry.	A	P
5. The animals started fighting.	S	M
6. The animals fought, but they stopped to take a breath.	L	T
7. A vulture was in a tree.	E	Z
8. Vultures eat dead things.	D	E
9. The lion looked at the boar.	F	D
10. The animals knew the vulture wanted to eat them, so they stopped fighting.	G	U
11. They did not want to be food for a vulture.	N	O
12. The boar asked the lion to drink first.	N	I
13. The animals shared the water, and they became friends.	P	Y

Look back at the activity on page 119. To solve the riddle, write each circled letter in order on the lines below.

Why did the lion spit out the clown?

Because ____ ____   ____ ____ ____ ____ ____ ____   ____ ____ ____ ____ ____!

Activity 2

Rewrite the compound sentence as two simple sentences.

"I am king of the jungle, so I will take the first drink!"

_____

_____

_____

_____

SHADES OF MEANING

If you were coloring a picture of a blue sky on a sunny day, you would probably choose a pretty bright blue color, wouldn't you? Just like choosing the right color would be important for your picture, selecting the right words for what you want to say is also very important.

Activity 1

Read the list of words below and match them to their similar meaning.

1. Read this sentence from the fable:

   "My tusks can **tear** an animal to shreds, so I will take the first drink."

   Which word has almost the same meaning as **tear**?

   A. slit

   B. rip

   C. scratch

2. What image does **smacked** make you think of?

_____

_____

_____

3. What if **spanked** was used instead of **smacked**? Would the image you have of the lion "smacking" the boar be different? Why or why not?

_____

_____

_____

Activity 2

Complete the sentences with the strongest word in the set.

1. Jeeneka was _____ when her kitty ran away. (heartbroken, sad, depressed)

2. Jaden was _____ when he won the art contest! (happy, glad, thrilled)

3. The universe is _____. (big, enormous, large)

4. My mom was _____ when I lost my sister at the store. (furious, cross, grumpy)

SHARE YOUR OPINION

Everyone has an opinion—which includes you! If you were the boar, would you have been friends with the lion? Tell why or why not.

Write it down! Be sure you have a topic sentence (or main idea) that tells your opinion. Next, list three reasons why you would or would not have been friends with the lion. Remember to use linking words (e.g., because, and, also) to connect your opinion and reasons. Remember to write a conclusion that sums up your ideas.

Topic sentence (Your opinion):

Reason 1:

Reason 2:

Reason 3:

Conclusion:

SHARE YOUR OPINION

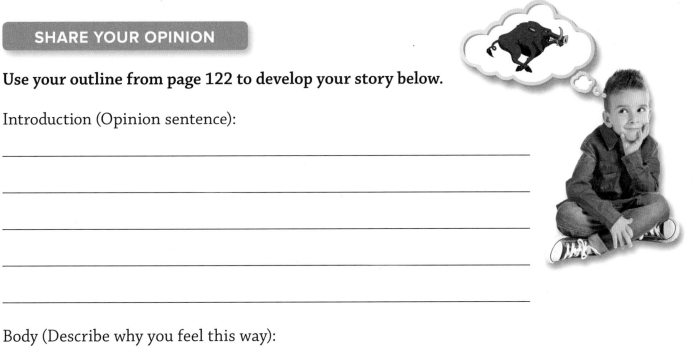

Use your outline from page 122 to develop your story below.

Introduction (Opinion sentence):

_____

_____

_____

_____

Body (Describe why you feel this way):

_____

_____

_____

_____

_____

_____

_____

Conclusion (Restate your opinion):

_____

_____

_____

_____

_____

Remember to use your *My Journal* **pages at the back of the workbook if you need more space to write.**

Fairytales

Fairytales are stories that are passed down from parents to their children year after year. Most fairytales are so old that no one knows who first came up with them, and many different people have written them down. Usually, fairytales teach a lesson or tell a story about something that many people can understand. They also deal with important issues, like the difference between good and evil. Usually, fairytales include supernatural or magical events and characters that could never exist in real life.

Sometimes, fairytales that are similar can be found in completely different cultures, or groups of people around the world. One of the oldest fairytales that can be found in almost every culture around the world is what most people in the United States would call the Cinderella story. In this unit, you will read two versions of the Cinderella fairytale and look at how they are the same and how they are different.

Cinderella

This version of Cinderella by Charles Perrault, from France, is the most popular version in the United States. It has been turned into many books and movies, and is the reason why we call stories that are similar "Cinderella stories." As you read, you may want to look up the **bold** words in a dictionary.

Once upon a time, a man had a young daughter but no wife. He got married to a woman who had two daughters. The new stepmother and stepdaughters were beautiful, but they were also mean and proud. They hated the man's daughter because she was so pretty and good. The stepmother made her do all the **chores** around the house. They started to call her Cinderella because she was always covered with the **cinders** from the fireplaces she had to clean.

One day the prince in Cinderella's town decided to have a grand **ball**. All of the girls in town were invited to go dance with the prince. Cinderella helped her stepsisters get ready for the party, but she was not allowed to go with them. "You are too dirty!" said her stepmother. "Everyone would laugh if they saw you at the palace." Cinderella tried to be brave. But as soon as her family left for the ball, she started to cry.

A fairy found her crying. "What is wrong?" she asked.

"I would like to go to the ball so much! But I cannot," Cinderella said. "I do not have anything nice to wear. My stepmother made me stay home."

The fairy knew just what to do. With a wave of her hand, she turned a pumpkin into a grand **carriage**. Then she changed six mice into fine horses to pull it, and made a rat into a driver. Cinderella was still wearing **filthy**, **ragged** clothing. The fairy waved her hand again and suddenly Cinderella was wearing a beautiful dress and lots of jewelry! Finally, she gave Cinderella a pair of glass slippers for her feet.

"Now you are ready for the ball," she said. "Have fun, but do not stay past midnight, because the magic will end!"

Cinderella went to the palace. She was the most beautiful girl at the party, and the prince danced with her more than all the other girls. Her stepmother and stepsisters did not even know who she was, because she was not covered in dirt and ashes!

She was having such a good time that she forgot to leave the ball early. Then the clock began to strike midnight. When Cinderella heard it, she stopped dancing and ran from the palace. She was in such a hurry that when one of her glass slippers came off, she left it behind! Just like the fairy said, the magic ended at the last stroke of midnight. The carriage, horses, and driver **vanished**. Cinderella was once again dressed in rags. Nothing was left except the one glass slipper the fairy had given her as a gift.

The next day, everyone in town was talking about the **mysterious** girl who danced with the prince and **disappeared** at midnight. The prince's **servants** tried to catch her, but they only found a dirty girl with a pumpkin. The only clue the prince had was a glass slipper the girl lost when she ran away.

The prince visited every girl in the town. He wanted to see which one the beautiful shoe fit. Many girls **claimed** to be the owner of the slipper, but their feet were always either too big or too small. Finally, the prince came to Cinderella's house. The stepsisters tried to put on the slipper. It did not fit. Cinderella knew it was her slipper, but she pretended she did not know anything about it.

glossary

Carriage: A wheeled vehicle drawn by a horse

Chores: Everyday work around the house

Claim: To state as fact

Cinders: A piece of partly burned wood

Vanished: To pass from sight

Mysterious: Something that cannot be explained

Servant: A person who performs household or personal services

"Can I please try it on?" she asked.

The stepsisters thought it was a silly idea. However, the prince could see that she was very pretty under all of the dirt. He let her try. The slipper fit! Just at that second, the fairy appeared again. She changed Cinderella's ragged clothes into another fine dress. Finally, the stepsisters and the prince could see that Cinderella was the same beautiful girl from the ball!

The prince and Cinderella got married. Cinderella went to live at the palace. She never had to clean a fireplace ever again. Even though she was now very rich and important, she did not punish her stepsisters. Instead, she helped them marry princes, too. All of them lived happily ever after.

Digging Deeper

Read other versions of the Cinderella story from around the world by visiting the link below:

kidworldcitizen.org/2012/10/11/cinderella-story-around-the-world

Then write about what happens to Cinderella and the Prince after they marry.

UNDERSTANDING THEME

For hundreds of years people have read fables, fairytales, and myths. Many of these stories were meant to teach a theme, moral, or lesson. We can figure out the central message or theme through key details in the text.

Use "Cinderella" to answer the following questions.

1. What is the **central theme** of the story?

   A. Bad things happen to bad people.

   B. Good things happen to good people.

   C. Beauty comes from the inside.

2. How does Cinderella treat her stepsisters at the end of the story?

   A. She treats them the same way they used to treat her.

   B. She moves to the palace and never thinks about them again.

   C. She is nice to them even though they were mean to her.

3. Why does the stepmother say that Cinderella cannot go to the ball?

   A. Cinderella did not finish all of her chores that day.

   B. Cinderella is too dirty from her chores to go to the ball.

   C. Cinderella has no nice clothes to wear to the ball.

4. Why does the prince let Cinderella try on the slipper?

   A. He thinks she is pretty.

   B. He does not like her stepsisters.

   C. He feels sorry for her.

5. What lesson can you learn from how Cinderella treats her stepsisters at the end of the story?

   _____

   _____

   _____

UNDERSTANDING POINT OF VIEW

Every character in a story has his, her, or its own thoughts and feelings—or **point of view**. As a reader, you need to be able to understand the different thoughts of each character. Usually everyone in a story has a different point of view, just like in real life!

Use "Cinderella" to answer the following questions.

Activity 1

1. How does Cinderella feel when her stepmother says she cannot go to the ball?

    A. afraid

    B. sad

    C. mad

2. How do Cinderella's stepmother and stepsisters feel about her?

    A. They feel sorry for her.

    B. They are proud of her.

    C. They are jealous of her.

Activity 2

What do you imagine Cinderella is thinking and feeling when she sees the fairy? How would you feel if you were Cinderella? List Cinderella's thoughts and your thoughts and feelings in the chart below.

Cinderella's Feelings and Thoughts

Your Feelings and Thoughts

SHADES OF MEANING

Many verbs and adjectives are closely related to one another. They have similar definitions, but have slightly different meanings.

> Examples: The girl **tossed** the ball.
>
> The girl **hurled** the ball.
>
> Hurled and tossed have similar but different meanings.
>
> **Toss** means to throw something gently and slowly.
>
> **Hurl** means to throw something with force.

Activity 1

Write a word that is closely related to the following verbs and adjectives from the story.

1. Filthy _____

   _____

2. Ragged _____

   _____

3. Pretty _____

   _____

4. Appeared _____

   _____

   _____

Activity 2

Look at the words below the glass slippers and the fairies. Draw a line from the words below the glass slippers that mean almost the same as the words below the fairies.

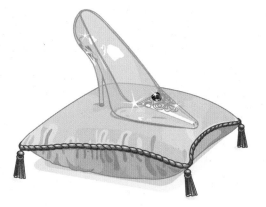

wicked

work

disappear

mean

chore

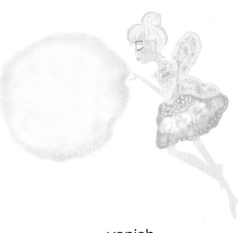

vanish

USING REFERENCE MATERIAL

A glossary or dictionary is a list of words in alphabetical order with explanations or definitions of words. It can be used to find the correct spelling and grammar usage for words. Glossaries are often found at the end of a book—especially books about science. The dictionary is your best reading tool! It helps you understand what a word means and find the correct spelling and grammar usage for words.

Read Cinderella's invitation to the ball. Circle the four misspelled words in the invitation. Use a dictionary to write the correct spellings on the lines below.

Dear Cinderella,

We are happy to announce that you have been invited to the royel ball on Augest 25, at 7pm. Dinner will be served before the dence. Prince Edgar is looking forwerd to meeting all the ladies in the kingdom. We hope you can attend.

Sincerely,
Prince Edgar

1. _____ 2. _____ 3. _____ 4. _____

Challenge: Using a dictionary, correct the misspelled words in the box below. Write another word for each that has almost the same meaning.

Cleen _____

Whispar _____

Petch _____

Nible _____

Abadeja, the Cinderella of the Philippines

Once upon a time, a beautiful girl named Abadeja lived in a village with her father, her stepmother, and three stepsisters. Abadeja's stepmother hated her because she was more beautiful than her own daughters. She made Abadeja do all the hardest jobs around the house.

One day, Abadeja's stepmother handed her two pieces of cloth, one white and one black. "Take these to the river," she said. "Wash them until the white one turns black and the black one turns white. If you do not, I will punish you."

Abadeja went to the river with the pieces of cloth and started to cry. Suddenly, a beautiful woman appeared. "What is wrong?" the woman asked. Abadeja told the woman about the impossible job she had to do. The woman touched the cloths. In just one second, the white one became black and the black one became white. "Come and see me whenever you need help," she said. Abadeja took the cloths home to her stepmother, and did not get punished.

The next day, a wild pig came into Abadeja's house and tore up a floor mat. Abadeja's stepmother handed her the torn mat. "You must make this mat as good as new, or I will punish you," she said. Abadeja went back down to the river with the mat, crying.

The beautiful woman appeared again. "I must make this mat as good as new," Abadeja told her. "It is impossible!" The woman took the mat and waved it in the air. It was like new again! She gave the mat back to Abadeja. She also gave Abadeja a beautiful pet chicken. Abadeja went home with the mat and the chicken. Abadeja's stepmother was very angry. She wanted to punish Abadeja but Abadeja had done what she asked!

The next day the stepmother was still angry. While Abadeja was working, her stepmother cooked the chicken for dinner. When Abadeja saw that her chicken was gone, she ran to the river. The beautiful woman met her again. "What should I do?" Abadeja cried. "My stepmother cooked the chicken!"

"Plant the feet of the chicken in the forest," the woman said.

Abadeja made a little garden deep in the forest and planted the chicken's feet. A month later, she went back to check on them. In the place where she planted the chicken's feet, two trees had grown! They were covered with fine jewelry and fancy clothes. Abadeja was happy, but she did not tell anyone about the garden. She did not want her stepmother to find out.

One day the son of the richest man in the village went on a walk in the forest. While he was walking, he found Abadeja's garden. He took a ring from one of the trees and put it on his finger. Suddenly it was stuck! The ring would not come off of his finger no matter how hard he pulled.

His father had an idea. "Let each girl in the village take the ring off of your finger," he said. "The one who can remove the ring will become your wife."

All of the girls tried except Abadeja. Her stepmother would not let her go try. But none of the other girls were able to remove the ring. Finally, the rich man found out that Abadeja had not tried yet. He ordered the stepmother to let her go and try. When Abadeja touched the ring, it slid off of the boy's finger right away. The next day, Abadeja and the son of the rich man got married. They lived happily for many years.

CHARACTERS RESPOND TO CHALLENGES

Characters in stories often face problems. Understanding a character's attitude and how they respond to challenges will help you better understand the story and the characters.

Use "Abadeja, the Cinderella of the Philippines" to answer the following questions.

1. Write at least one problem that each character has in the story.

    A. Abadeja

    _____

    B. The stepmother

    _____

    C. The rich man's son

    _____

2. Pick one of the characters from the story to answer the questions below.

    A. Does the character solve, or fix, the problem?

    _____

    B. Did they need help, or did they try to fix it themselves?

    _____

3. Why did Abadeja start to cry when she was at the river with the two pieces of cloth?

    A. She did not know how to wash the two pieces of cloth.
    B. She was afraid of the strange woman who appeared.
    C. She knew her stepmother's orders were impossible.

4. Why did the rich man marry Abadeja?

    A. He felt sorry for her.
    B. Her family was rich.
    C. She removed his ring.

UNDERSTANDING POINT OF VIEW

When you read a story, you are reading it from your point of view. The person who wrote it has his or her point of view. The characters in the story have points of view, too!

Use "Abadeja, the Cinderella of the Philippines" to answer the following questions.

1. How do you think Abadeja feels about the woman?

   A. She is jealous of her.

   B. She is angry with her.

   C. She is grateful for her.

2. How would you feel toward the stepmother if you were Abadeja? _____

   _____

   _____

   _____

3. What is the stepmother's point of view of Abadeja?

   A. She thinks Abadeja is lazy.

   B. She thinks Abadeja is beautiful.

   C. She thinks the father favors Abadeja.

4. Pick another character from the story: _____

   What is that character's point of view? In other words, what does that character think and feel about the other characters and the things that happen in the story?

   _____

   _____

   _____

   _____

COMPARE AND CONTRAST

When you compare and contrast two or more things, you are trying to find out how they are alike or how they are different. When there is more than one version of a story, you may be able to see how characters, events, and themes in those stories are alike or different.

1. After reading "Cinderella" and "Abadeja, the Cinderella of the Philippines," describe how the stories are **similar**. Fill in the chart below.

Cinderella	Abadeja

2. After reading Cinderella and "Abadeja, the Cinderella of the Philippines," describe how the stories are **different**. Fill in the chart below.

Cinderella	Abadeja

WRITE YOUR EXPLANATION

An explanatory text is written to explain how or why something happens. An explanatory text should have a strong introduction to grab the reader's attention and plenty of supporting facts and details to support the main idea, or topic of the story. A strong ending, or conclusion, is needed to bring everything together, restate the key details, and close the writing.

Have you ever helped someone that you felt sorry for? Pretend you helped someone solve a problem. What is their problem? Do you know the person, or are they a stranger? What will you do to help this person solve their problem?

Introduction (Topic sentence stating the main idea):

Event 1 (Supporting Detail):

Event 2 (Supporting Detail):

Event 3 (Supporting Detail):

Conclusion (paragraph that summarizes the main idea):

Poetry

Poetry is a special kind of writing. You might think of it as a song without the music. Music has a rhythm (RITH-um), or pattern of movement. Poetry does, too! But instead of the rhythm coming from music, it comes from the way the words and phrases are put together. A single piece of poetry is called a poem. There are different kinds of poems about almost anything you can imagine! Some poems tell stories; others do not. Poems can be happy, sad, silly... there are even poems made of nonsense words! In this unit, you will practice reading and understanding poetry. You will also see how poetry is different from other kinds of writing.

The Swing

by Robert Louis Stevenson

How do you like to go up in a swing,
   Up in the air so blue?
Oh, I do think it the pleasantest thing
4   Ever a child can do!

Up in the air and over the wall,
   Till I can see so wide,
Rivers and trees and cattle and all
8   Over the countryside—

Till I look down on the garden green,
   Down on the roof so brown—
Up in the air I go flying again,
12   Up in the air and down!

UNDERSTANDING KEY DETAILS

Use "The Swing" to answer the following questions.

1. What is the first thing the author sees when he goes over the wall?

   A. a garden

   B. a roof

   C. a river

2. In order to see "all over the countryside," the writer of the poem has to swing:

   A. high enough to see over a wall

   B. high enough to look down on the roof

   C. high enough to feel like he is flying

3. Reread the following line from the poem:

   "Till I can see so wide—"

   What does the author mean by this statement?

   _____

   _____

4. Reread the following line from the poem:

   "Down on the roof so brown—"

   What does this most likely suggest?

   A. The child is swinging fast.

   B. The child is swinging high.

   C. The child is swinging low.

5. Name other animals a person might see in the country.

   _____

   _____

   _____

UNDERSTANDING RHYTHM

The **rhythm**, or pattern of movement, in this poem comes from the way that the words and phrases (groups of words) are put together. As you probably noticed, this poem is not written in the same kinds of sentences and paragraphs that you would find in a prose (non-poetry) story. One of the special ways that poets create rhythm and movement with words is by using rhyming words. Words that rhyme sound the same.

For example, the words **head** and **bed** are rhyming words.

Use "The Swing" to answer the following questions.

Stanza:
A section of a poem made up of a series of lines that usually repeat a pattern of rhythm and rhyme.

1. What phrase do you see repeated in the poem?

    A. Up in the air

    B. Down on the roof

    C. Over the countryside

2. What **rhyming** words can you find in the poem?

    _____

    _____

    _____

3. Where did you find the rhyming lines in this poem?

    A. At the end of every line

    B. At the beginning of every other line

    C. At the end of every other line

4. Think of another group of lines or **stanza** for the poem. Write it on the lines below.

    _____

    _____

    _____

    _____

PICTURES HELP EXPLAIN A TEXT

Use "The Swing" to answer the following questions.

1. Look at the picture next to the poem. Which line from the poem best matches what you see in the picture?

   A. "Up in the air and over the wall"

   B. "Up in the air so blue"

   C. "Up in the air I go flying again"

2. Look at the boy in the picture. Do you think he would agree with the poet's feelings about swinging? Why or why not? Use details from the picture and the poem in your answer.

   _____

   _____

   _____

   _____

   _____

3. Think about the **setting** of the poem.

   A. Look at the picture. Where do you think the swing is located?

   _____

   _____

   B. What helped you figure out where the swing is located?

   _____

   _____

   _____

   _____

UNDERSTANDING THE CLUES

You will practice using context clues to understand words from the poem. You can look at the words before or after the word you do not know as clues to help figure out its meaning.

> Example: Because the game was **complicated**, we read the instructions so we could understand what to do.
>
> How can you figure out what the word complicated means? Well, the words "instructions so we could understand what to do" tells you that complicated means something that must be very hard to understand.

Use "The Swing" to answer the following questions.

1. Find the word **pleasantest** in the poem. What do you think the word pleasantest means?

   _____

   _____

2. Which words or ideas from the poem helped you come up with your definition of pleasantest? Explain how you made your definition in the space below.

   _____

   _____

3. Read this stanza from the poem and circle the three words in the stanza that give a clue to the meaning of the word **countryside**.

   > Up in the air and over the wall,
   >   Till I can see so wide,
   > Rivers and trees and cattle and all
   >   Over the countryside—

4. What is the definition of countryside?

   _____

   _____

UNDERSTANDING REAL-LIFE CONNECTIONS IN WRITING

When you learn new words, it is good to connect them to things you already know. When you think about how a word is connected to different things in your own life, you are more likely to remember the word in the future and understand what it means more easily.

Use "The Swing" to answer the following questions.

1. Which is **pleasantest**?

   A. Going to the dentist

   B. Swimming in a pool

   C. Doing household chores

2. What are some of the pleasantest things that you can think of?

   _____

   _____

   _____

   _____

3. Think about the definition of the word **countryside**. Do you live in the countryside? Is the countryside near your home? Explain how you know whether you live in or close to the countryside.

   _____

   _____

   _____

   _____

4. What is an example of something you would find in the countryside?

   A. A playground

   B. A large field of flowers

   C. An apartment building

WRITE YOUR NARRATIVE

A **narrative** is a piece of writing that tells a story. In this section, you will create your own short **narrative** about swinging. What story will you tell?

Characters	Setting	Plot
Who is the story about? Have at least two main characters identified.	When and where does the story take place? Is it summertime? Wintertime? What state or country will you choose?	What are the events in the story? What adventures await your characters? Use your imagination!

_____

_____

_____

_____

_____

_____

_____

_____

_____

_____

Conclusion: How does your story end?

REVIEW

Reading Fluency

Adults: Time your student for one minute while he or she is reading to you. Make a note of where he or she is after one minute to track your student's fluency. (Your student should be able to read 60–90 words per minute). Then, have your student continue reading to the end of the story and answer the questions that follow.

Kasim's Unlucky Shoes
A Middle Eastern Folktale

Long ago a man named Kasim lived in the city of Basra. Kasim was rich, but he never spent   19
any money. He wore very old shoes because he did not want to buy new ones for himself.   37
The shoes had been repaired many times. There were big nails holding the bottoms on and   53
lots of patches on the tops. They were heavy and looked very strange. Everyone in the city   70
knew about them.   73

One day Kasim went to the pool. He met a friend on the way. "You should buy   90
yourself a new pair of shoes," his friend said. "Everyone in the city makes fun of your   107

ancient shoes."   109

"They are fine. I can keep wearing them," Kasim   118
said. He went on his way to the pool. He left his   130
shoes outside and went swimming. But afterward,   137
he could not find his old shoes. He only saw a   148
pair of new shoes. Kasim did not know that an   158
important judge was also at the pool. He thought   167
that his friend was trying to surprise him with new   177
shoes. He put them on and went home.   185

When the judge came out of the pool, he could   195
not find his new shoes! He only saw Kasim's old   205
shoes. It looked like Kasim had stolen the judge's shoes. Kasim explained that it was   220
a mistake, but he still had to pay a fine so he would not go to jail. Kasim was so upset   241
about the fine that he threw his old shoes in the river.   253

The next day a fisherman pulled the shoes up in his fishing net. The nails in the   270
shoes had ripped huge holes in the net! The fisherman was angry. He went to Kasim's   286

house and threw the shoes through the window. When Kasim saw the broken window	300
and that the shoes were back again, he was upset. "Now I have to pay for a new window,"	319
he said. "I must get rid of these shoes for good!"	330

Kasim took the shoes far away from the city and dropped them in a lake. But the lake was connected to the city by a water pipe. A few days later the pipe stopped working. When some repair men looked in the pipe, they found Kasim's shoes blocking it. The judge made Kasim pay even more money to repair the pipe.

Kasim took the shoes far away from the city and dropped them in a lake. But the	347
lake was connected to the city by a water pipe. A few days later the pipe stopped working.	365
When some repair men looked in the pipe, they found Kasim's shoes blocking it. The	380
judge made Kasim pay even more money to repair the pipe.	391
"No more!" Kasim finally said to the judge. "I used to be a rich man, and now I am	410
poor just from paying for all the problems caused by my shoes! I have learned my lesson."	427
Kasim never kept a pair of shoes for such a long time ever again.	441

Words read in 1 minute − errors = WPM

Use "Kasim's Unlucky Shoes" to answer the following questions.

Activity 1

Practice using reflexive pronouns.

1. Which of the following sentences from the story contains a **reflexive pronoun**?

    A. "Long ago a man named Kasim lived in the city of Baghdad."

    B. "Everyone in the city knew about them"

    C. "You should buy yourself a new pair of shoes."

2. Circle the reflexive pronoun in the following sentence from the story:

    "He wore very old shoes because he did not want to buy new ones for himself."

Activity 2

Use what you learned about simple and compound sentences to answer the questions on the next page.

1. Read the following sentence from the story:

    "I used to be a rich man, and now I am poor just from paying for all the problems caused by my shoes!"

A. What kind of sentence is this? Circle the correct response:

Simple   Compound

B. In the space provided, divide the sentence into two new sentences:

_____

_____

2. Read the following sentence from the story:

"Kasim never kept a pair of shoes for such a long time ever again."

Rearrange the sentence so that it has a different subject but still says the same thing.

_____

_____

Activity 3

Use context clues to figure out the meaning of the bolded words in the following questions.

1. Reread the first paragraph of the story. Based on the other information in the paragraph, what does the word **repaired** mean, and how do you know?

_____

_____

2. Read the following sentence:

*"Kasim explained that it was a mistake, but he still had to pay a **fine** so he would not go to jail."*

Based on the other information in the sentence, which definition, or meaning, of "fine" is being used here?

A. In good health or condition
B. Money charged as a punishment
C. Very thin, delicate

Activity 4

Connect the words from the story to real life. Then, tell how they are the same and different from each other.

1. Look back at the way Kasim's shoes are described in the story.

    How are Kasim's shoes described?

    _____

    _____

    _____

    What else would you describe as **strange**? (*Hint:* What does the word strange mean to you? What do you think looks strange, and why?)

    _____

    _____

    _____

2. Kasim's shoes are **old**. What other word used to describe Kasim's shoes means almost, but not quite, the same as **old**?

    A. Strange

    B. Heavy

    C. Ancient

3. Describe something you have that is strange or old.

    _____

    _____

    _____

    _____

The Little Turtle

by Vachel Lindsay

There was a little turtle.
He lived in a box.
He swam in a puddle.
4   He climbed on the rocks.

He snapped at a mosquito.
He snapped at a flea.
He snapped at a minnow.
8   And he snapped at me.

He caught the mosquito.
He caught the flea.
He caught the minnow.
12   But he didn't catch me.

Activity 1

Use what you know about characters and settings to answer the following questions.

1. Who are the main characters in the poem?

    _____

    _____

2. Does this poem have a setting, or place where the main action happens? If it does, what is the setting? If it does not, why not?

    _____

    _____

    _____

3. Which two verbs, or action words, used to describe the turtle are most important to the poem?

    A. snapped and caught

    B. lived and snapped

    C. swam and climbed

Activity 2

Use what you know about the structure of poems to answer the following questions.

1. Write two pairs of rhyming words from the poem in the spaces below:

    _____   _____

    _____   _____

2. What phrases, or groups of words, does the writer of the poem repeat?

    _____

    _____

3. How do you know that this is a poem, and not prose (writing that is not poetry)? (*Hint:* Think about the rhythm and structure of the piece of writing, or how the poem is put together.)

_____

_____

_____

4. What is the purpose of the first stanza, or section, of the poem? What is the poet doing in this part of the poem?

_____

_____

5. Where does the main action of the poem begin, and what is the first thing that happens in the main action of the poem?

_____

_____

6. What happens last in the poem?

_____

_____

Activity 3

Use what you know about point of view to answer the following questions.

1. Whose point of view is the poem being told from? (Who is telling what happens in the poem?)

    A. The little turtle

    B. The writer of the poem

    C. The reader of the poem

2. How do you think the little turtle feels about the other main character in the poem, "me"? Explain your answer in the space provided.

    _____

    _____

3. The main characters in the poem probably have very different points of view about the other animals mentioned in the poem.

    A. How do you think the little turtle feels about the mosquito, the flea, and the minnow?

    _____

    _____

    B. How do you think the poet (or any other human) would feel about the mosquito, the flea, and the minnow?

    _____

    _____

Activity 4

Look at the picture of a turtle above. In the poem, the little turtle is described as living "in a box." Based on your knowledge and the information in the picture, what is the "box" that the turtle lives in? What makes it box-like?

_____

_____

_____

_____

DISCOVER

Write Your Narrative

Have you enjoyed reading the fairytales and folktales in this book? Although each story was different, you might have noticed that they also had things in common, such as having a beginning, characters, a problem, and an ending. You might think of those things as the basic building blocks of a story. In this section, you will write a story of your own.

First, you need to decide what your story will be about. Will it be something that actually happened or a made-up event? Will it be a mixture of real and made-up events?

Outline the building blocks of your story below. Your ideas should be very short, maybe just a few words or a single sentence. Use the template on the following page to organize your thoughts.

Characters	Setting	Plot
Who is the story about?	When does the story take place? Where does the story take place?	What are the events in the story? What adventures await your characters? Use your imagination!

WRITE YOUR NARRATIVE

Create a plot:

What happens first ...

Next ...

Then ...

Finally ... How does your story end?

My Journal

My Journal

My Journal

My Journal

Answer Key

Reading: Foundational Skills

Unit 1—Recognizing Phonics and Words
Lesson 1—Short and Long Vowel Sounds
Page 14. Activity 1: 1. A; 2. A; Activity 2: 1. cliff; 2. pet; 3. stop; 4. rub; Activity 3: white, tree, name, so, Steve

Lesson 2—Vowel Teams
Page 15. Activity 1: 1. b; 2. c; 3. a; Activity 2: 1. new, coat, school; 2. grew, blue; 3. wait, tree; 4. eat, play

Page 16. Activity 3: 1. glue; 2. soap; 3. read; 4. pool; Activity 4: 1. Answers will vary. Examples: head, heed, and hood; 2. Answers will vary. Examples: feel, foal, and fool; 3. Answers will vary. Examples: heal and heel; 4. Answers will vary. Examples: beat, beet, and boot

Lesson 3—Long Vowel Sounds in Two-Syllable Words
Page 17. Activity 1: 1. C; 2. A; Activity 2: 1. day; 2. home; 3. bee; Challenge: hero, invites, maybe

Lesson 4—Prefixes and Suffixes
Page 18. Activity 1: a lock that is opened; 2. full of hope; 3. full of care

Page 19. Activity 2: 1. c; 2. d; 3. b; 4. a; Activity 3: 1. teacher; 2. unhappy; 3. replay; 4. smallest

Lesson 5—Homophones
Page 20. Activity 1: 1. You're, your; 2. inn, in; Activity 2: 1. C; 2. A

Page 21. Activity 3: 1. It's, its; 2. knew, new; 3. deer, dear; 4. scent, cent; Activity 4: 1. d; 2. a; 3. b; 4. c; Activity 5: Answers will vary. 1. Example: We are going to sail our ship on the ocean. Mom said she would buy me a bike once it goes on sale. 2. Example: My dad likes to eat meat and potatoes. I am going to meet my friend at the swimming pool.

Lesson 6—Irregular Words
Page 22. Activity 1: 1. d; 2. c; 3. a; 4. b; Activity 2: 1. diamond; 2. knife; 3. islands; 4. should

Page 23. Activity 3: 1. glove; 2. heart; 3. young; 4. friend;

Activity 4: 1. iron, knock, dough, know, eighty, captain; 2. Answers will vary. Possible answers: Captain Joe wears a blue coat. My friend has eighty baseball cards.

Unit 2—Fluency: Read with Purpose and Understanding
Lesson 1—Science at the Park
Page 27. Guided Questions: 1. in the backyard or a nearby park; 2. A field guide is a person who helps another person to look more closely at nature by explaining and naming living things; 3. Rachel has invited the students back during the fall to see how the environment changes when the season changes. She specifically wants to pay special attention to caterpillars; 4. Answers will vary. Example: Jaquan is thrilled at the idea of seeing the caterpillar's growth. He also is very excited to tell his brother about other cool science facts that he learned that he did not speak about in the letter.

Lesson 2—Sparky the Guide Dog
Page 29. Guided Questions: 1. Annabelle needs Sparky to help her walk and keep her safe; 2. Taught to do something, such as obey commands; 3. Sparky would try and get Annabelle out of harm's way as quickly as possible; 4. Guide dogs must try to stay away from things that may take their attention away from their owners, so they sometimes do not like to be petted or take treats.

Lesson 3—Let's Recycle!
Page 31. Guided Questions: 1. Unwanted trash outlives humans and can cause harm to ocean animals; 2. B; 3. collecting garbage, making old materials into new material, and buying recycled items; 4. The author includes a website for additional information: *www.ecy.wa.gov*.

Lesson 4—How to Paper Mâché
Page 33. 1. It helps kids learn about colors, words, and actions; 2. Paper mâché means chewed paper; 3. One list has the ingredients for the glue mixture, while the other list has art supplies needed to finish the project; 4. The author includes step-by-step instructions for the process,

and there is a picture at the beginning of the passage that shows the tools needed.

Reading and Writing: Informational Texts

Unit 3—How Flowers and Plants Grow
Lesson 1—Amazing Plants

Page 38. Finding the Main Idea and Details: 1. A; 2. A; 3. C; 4. A

Page 39. Describing Scientific Ideas: Roots: take in water and nutrients for the plant, hold the plant in the ground; Stem: Carries nutrients from the root to all other plant parts, helps plant stand tall and strong; Leaves: use air, water, and sun to make food for the plant; Flower: holds the part of the plant that reproduces or makes new plants.

Page 40. Understanding the Clues: 1. B; 2. food, water, vitamins, minerals; 3. C; 4. My body needs to store energy so I can grow tall and strong and so I can be healthy. It also helps me do things I like such as playing and going to school.

Page 41. Using Nouns and Adjectives: 1. Plant stems, trunk, tree; 2. soft, thin; 3. B; 4. A

Lesson 2—The Cycle of Life

Page 45. Finding the Main Idea and Details: 1. C; 2. C; 3. Insects carry the pollen to other plants so they can start making seeds for new plants to grow; 4. Fruit will become ripe and fall off a tree. The fruit will rot on the ground so the seeds are free to go into the ground. With the help of water, sunlight, soil, and air, the seeds get buried. The seed sprouts and becomes a seedling. A new plant has been created.

Page 46. Vocabulary Development: 1. C; 2. A; Shades of Meaning: 3. B; 4. A

Page 47. Comparing and Contrasting Articles: 1. Answers will vary. Examples: The articles are similar because they discuss what a plant needs to be healthy, and make new plants or reproduce. In both articles the plants depend on water and soil for the process of nutrition and reproduction. The articles are different because one talks more about how plants are made and the other talks about nourishing a growing plant.

Unit 4—Animals With and Without Backbones
Lesson 1—Bony

Page 51. Finding the Main Idea and Details: 1. C; 2. C; Author's Purpose: 1. B

Page 53. Using Past Tense Verbs: 1. A; 2. hid, ran; 3. sat, ate, told; Using Adverbs: 1. loudly; 2. slowly; 3. quietly; 4. quickly; 5. happily

Page 54. Prefixes: 1. unhappy, sad; 2. rewrite, write again; Shades of Meaning: 1. B; 2. A; 3. C; 4. discard; 5. leave

Lesson 2—Spineless

Page 56. Finding the Main Idea and Details: 1. C; 2. A; 3. B; 4. B

Page 57. Using Reference Material: 1. B; 2. B

Page 58. Comparing and Contrasting Articles: 1. Answers will vary. Possible answers: The articles are similar because they both discuss the features of invertebrates and vertebrates and the different animals that are invertebrates and vertebrates. Each article tells how certain kinds of animals look and behave. They are different because "Bony" talks about animals that have a backbone and "Spineless" talks about animals without a backbone.

Page 59. Using Apostrophes: Activity 1: 1. don't; 2. They're; 3. that's; Activity 2: 1. lobster's; 2. sponge's; 3. earthworm's

Stop and Think! Units 1–4 Review

Page 63. Activity 1: 1. swam; 2. held; 3. crawled; Activity 2: 1. quickly; 2. closely; 3. slowly. Activity 3: 1. lizard's; 2. iguana's; 3. tourist's. Activity 4: big, huge, great, grand

Stop and Think! Units 1–4 Understand

Page 65. 1. Spiders use their web as a safety net to catch them if they fall, like a net. 2. B; 3. C; 4. A

Unit 5—Special People in American History
Lesson 1—Sequoyah's Gift

Page 71. Author's Purpose: C; Pictures Help Explain a Text: C

Page 73. Comparing Formal and Informal Language: Activity 1: 1. I; 2. F; 3. I; 4. I; 5. F; Activity 2: change we're to we are, change 15 to fifteen, remove "Dude, that is so cool!"

Page 74. Using Glossaries and Dictionaries: Activity 1: 1. respect; 2. communicate; 3. Changing words from one language to another; Activity 2: 1. Cherokee; 2. Alphabet; 3. Symbol; 4. Indian; Challenge: Any formal written letter that uses words from the glossary is sufficient.

Lesson 2—Ride!

Page 78. Using Text Features: 1. A; 2. B; 3. B

Page 79. Author's Purpose: 1. C; 2. In 2001, she started a company called Sally Ride Science to encourage young people (mostly girls) to stick with science and math in school; 3. When Sally entered NASA in 1978 she had to complete very hard training.

Page 80. Using Reference Material: 1. B; 2. C

Page 81. Collective Nouns: 1. crew; 2. family; 3. company Adjectives: 1. bright; 2. difficult; 3. heavy

Unit 6—Historical Landmarks
Lesson 1—Mt. Rushmore

Page 88. Understanding Text Features: Activity 1: 1. B; 2. A; 3. C; 4. A; 5. B; 6. C

Page 89. Activity 2: chipmunk: caption; A Grand Idea: subheading; *www.nps.gov/Mt Rushmore:* hyperlink

Page 90. Irregular Plural Nouns: 1. fish; fish. There were seventeen fish in the tank; 2. foot; feet. My feet were sore from walking all day; 3. child; children. The children enjoyed their visit to the museum. (kid; kids also accepted)

Page 91. Using Commas in Greetings and Closings of Letters: 1. A; 2. C; 3. A

Page 92. Activity 2: Check that all commas are circled in the letter; 1. A; 2. A

Page 93. Challenge: Answers will vary.

Stop and Think! Units 5–6 Review

Page 95. Activity 1: 1. Wouldn't it be awesome to visit the Empire State Building? (informal) 2. We are looking forward to our field trip to the Empire State Building in three days. (formal) Activity 2: Students will create a glossary using the words listed. Activity 3: 1. group; 2. load

Page 96. Activity 4: 1. Answers will vary. Example: amazing, popular; 2. Answers will vary. Example: beautiful, sparkling; Activity 5: 1. amazing; 2. A very tall building with many stories; Activity 6: people, lives

Page 97. Activity 7: 1. Dear Mr. Lamb,; 2. Your buddy,; Activity 8: scared, grape; Activity 9: Any two goals the student writes about will be sufficient.

Stop and Think! Units 5–6 Understand

Page 100. 1. Space Flight Medal; 2. Outstanding Leadership Medal; 3. four; 4. Following Dreams; 5. Ellen Ochoa's

Childhood; 6. C; 7. Answers will vary. Possible answers: She followed her dreams and went on to become the first Hispanic woman astronaut in the world. Luckily, she did not let what others said stop her from following her dreams. As a result, when she grew up she became a mother, inventor, and the first Hispanic woman to ever go into space. NASA denied her application but she did not give up hope. Five years later she applied again and got the job in 1991.

Page 101. 8. NASA hired the first woman astronaut, Sally Ride. This along with her interest in engineering and space exploration research inspired her to apply for the astronaut program; 9. B; 10. C

Unit 7—Diversity in Cultures
Lesson 1—The King Who Caught a Thief

Page 109. Central Theme and Characters: 1. A; 2. The man was not content with getting his money back. He insisted that the king should punish the thief; 3. It tells me that the man was greedy and ungrateful because the king had already done a lot for him but he still was not satisfied. Also he was not a nice man because he wanted to see the other person get punished; 4. The king does not punish the thief like the man wants him to. He has his servants take the money outside the palace so the man has to go get it and leave; 5. The story is trying to say that you should not be greedy. The man is greedy because he keeps all of the riches for himself. The thief is greedy and steals the riches. The thief learns his lesson and is not greedy, so the king does not punish him. The man does not learn the lesson, so the king does not help him anymore.

Page 110. Looking at Story Structure: 1. A; 2. B; 3. B; 4. The king believes that the man is greedy. He does not care for the man.

Page 111. Making Connections with Pictures: 1. The man; 2. I know it is the man because he is sitting near a town like the man in the story. He is holding a necklace that is probably a gift that someone gave to him because he was sitting there.

Page 112. Pronouns: 1. A. himself; B. the man; 2. "I am not really poor," he said. "I have been keeping all the money for myself." myself

Page 113. Using Capital Letters: 1. A; B. 2. Ganges River

Unit 8—Messages and Morals
Lesson 1—The Lion and the Boar

Page 117. Central Message and Characters: 1. C; 2. C; 3. A vulture was waiting for one of them to lose the battle so it could eat the loser; 4. They decide to stop fighting and become friends.

Page 118. Parts of a Story: 1. One of the animals would have died and the vulture would have eaten the dead animal; 2. B; 3. Yes, the moral would no longer be "Watch out for those who will benefit from your loss," because the vulture is the one who wanted to benefit from the lion and boar's argument; 4. A

Page 119. Simple and Compound Sentences: Activity 1: 1. H; 2. E; 3. T; 4. A; 5. S; 6. T; 7. E; 8. D; 9. F; 10. U; 11. N; 12. N; 13. Y

Page 120. Riddle: He Tasted Funny! Activity 2: 1. "I am king of the jungle. I will take the first drink!"; Shades of Meaning: Activity 1: 1. B

Page 121. 2. To slap someone with an open hand or paw; 3. Answers will vary. Possible answers: Yes. Spanking makes me think of someone using an open hand to hit someone several times. Smacked makes me think of someone being slapped one time; Activity 2: 1. heartbroken; 2. thrilled; 3. enormous; 4. furious

Unit 9—Fairytales
Lesson 1—Cinderella

Page 128. Understanding Theme: 1. B; 2. C; 3. B; 4. A; 5. When someone is mean to you, you do not have to be mean to them back. You can be nice to them instead, and everyone can be happy.

Page 129. Understanding Point of View: Activity 1: 1. B; 2. C

Page 130. Activity 2: Answers will vary. Example: Cinderella may feel shocked and afraid when she first sees the fairy. Once the fairy speaks she probably feels happy and thankful. Answers will vary on how the child would feel.

Page 131. Shades of Meaning: Activity 1: Answers will vary. 1. Dirty; 2. Torn; 3. Beautiful; 4. Arrived

Page 132. Activity 2: wicked–mean, disappear–vanish, chore–work

Page 133. Using Reference Material: 1. royal; 2. August; 3. dance; 4. forward; Challenge: clean, whisper, pitch, nibble; Possible Answers: neat, talk, throw, chew

Lesson 2—Abadeja, the Cinderella of the Philippines

Page 136. Characters Respond to Challenges: Answers will vary. 1. (Abadeja): Her stepmother does not like her, wants to punish her, is mean to her, etc. She has to do impossible tasks like turning cloths different colors and making ruined floor mats as good as new; (Stepmom) Abadeja is more beautiful than her own daughters. Abadeja keeps finishing her jobs so she cannot punish her even though she really wants to; (Rich man's son) He has a ring stuck on his finger. None of the girls in town can get the ring off of his finger; 2. A. Yes/No Answers will vary; 2. B. Yes/No Answers will vary; 3. C; 4. C

Page 137. Understanding Point of View: 1. C; 2. Answers will vary. Example: I would be scared of my stepmother and angry with her; 3. B; 4. Answers will vary. Example: (The woman) The woman wants to help Abadeja. She is nice and she knows that Abadeja's stepmother is mean to her. She makes sure that good things happen to Abadeja so she can be happy. (The rich man's son) The rich man's son does not think about the other characters. He just wants to get the ring off of his finger, so he is only thinking about himself. (The rich man) The rich man is only worried about his son. He helps Abadeja but not because he likes her. He just wants the ring to come off of his son's finger.

Page 138. Compare and Contrast: Similar: they are both about a wicked stepmother who is mean to her stepdaughter, they both include a fairy woman who helps the girl, they both include a prince who marries the girl. Different: The setting is different, Cinderella goes to a ball, Abadeja removes a ring from the prince, etc.

Unit 10—Poetry
Lesson 1—The Swing

Page 142. Understanding Key Details: 1. C; 2. A; 3. Answers will vary. Example: This means that he or she would have a clear view all around. 4. B; 5. Answers will vary. Examples: horses, sheep, dogs, cats

Page 143. Understanding Rhythm: 1. A; 2. Swing, thing, wall, all, blue, do, wide, countryside, brown, down; 3. C; 4. Any stanza where every other line rhymes is acceptable.

Page 144. Pictures Help Explain a Text: 1. B; 2. Answers will vary. Possible answer: Yes, I think he would agree with the poet because the poet likes swinging. The boy is swinging high so he probably likes swinging, too; 3A.

Answers will vary. Possible answer: near a wall on the edge of town, in someone's yard, near a house or apartment building, in a small city or town; B. I think it is near a house or apartment because the person swinging can look down on the garden and the roof. It is probably their garden and the roof of the house or apartment. The wall that they see over could be the fence around the yard of the house, or apartment buildings.

Page 145. Understanding the Clues: 1. Answers will vary, but will most likely be positive in nature. Possible answer: I think "pleasantest" means "nicest"; 2. A sample answer follows for the definition "nicest": I think that the word "pleasantest" means "nicest" because the poem is about how much the poet likes swinging so it has to be a good word; 3. rivers, trees, cattle; 4. "Countryside" is the place outside of cities.

Page 146. Real-Life Connections: 1. B; 2. The student's answer will be the product of personal opinion, but should be something that can be recognized as positive or pleasant in nature; 3. The student's answer will be the product of personal experience, but the explanation should reflect an understanding of what "countryside" means as defined in earlier questions and compare/contrast the student's own living arrangements to that definition; 4. B

Stop and Think! Units 7–10 Review

Page 149. Activity 1: 1. C; 2. himself

Page 150. Activity 2: 1A. Compound, B. I used to be a rich man. Now I am poor just from paying for all the problems caused by my shoes! 2. A pair of shoes was never kept for such a long time by Kasim ever again; Activity 3: 1. Repaired probably means fixed. It says that there were big nails holding the bottoms on, so the bottoms probably fell off and he had to fix them by nailing them back on. Patches are also used for fixing things that have holes in them; 2. B

Page 151. Activity 4: 1. Answers should include some or all of the following: Very old, repaired many times, nails holding the bottoms on, patches on the tops, heavy, strange-looking. Possible answer: Strange is not normal, or odd looking; 2. C; 3. Possible answer: I have an old pair of jeans with rips and tears in them.

Stop and Think! Units 7–10 Understand

Page 153. Activity 1: 1. The poet, turtle, me; 2. Answers will vary: Sample answer: Yes, the setting is near a pond or another body of water because the poem says that the turtle swims and climbs on rocks. The turtle also snaps at a minnow, which is a fish, so the poem must take place near the water. No, there is no setting specifically mentioned in the poem. The introduction of the poem tells where the turtle lives, but the writer does not tell you where the main action of the poem takes place. 3. A; Activity 2: 1. Box and rocks, Flea and me; 2. He snapped, He caught

Page 154. 3. Answers will vary. Possible answer: I know that this is a poem because it is not like regular writing or talking. The sentences are arranged into verses instead of paragraphs. It also has rhythm or movement because of the way the lines are read and the rhyming words at the end of every other line; 4. Answers will vary. Example: In the first part of the poem, the poet is telling you some facts about the little turtle. This is the beginning of the poem, and the poet is introducing you to the other main character by telling you about the turtle; 5. The main action of the poem starts in the second verse of the poem, when the turtle snaps at a mosquito; 6. The turtle snaps at the person but does not catch the person; Activity 3: 1. B

Page 155. 2. Answers will vary. Example: The turtle thinks that the person "me" is food, because it snaps at the person the same as it snaps at a bug or a fish. The turtle is probably scared of the person "me" in the poem because the person is watching it eat these other animals, but a person is much bigger than a turtle; 3A. Answers will vary. Example: I think that the turtle thinks of the mosquito, the flea, and the minnow as food, because it snaps at those animals and catches them. B. Answers will vary. Example: The answer will most likely involve the main (human) character thinking about the secondary animal characters as lesser and/or annoying creatures; Activity 4: Answers will vary, but should include the fact that the "box" mentioned by the poet is the turtle's shell. The explanations may include: The shell is hard like a box. The shell has edges like a box. The shell protects the turtle like a box can protect whatever is inside it.

GRADES 2–6
TEST PRACTICE
for Common Core

With Common Core Standards being implemented across America, it's important to give students, teachers, and parents the tools they need to achieve success. That's why Barron's has created the *Core Focus* series. These multi-faceted, grade-specific workbooks are designed for self-study learning, and the units in each book are divided into thematic lessons that include:

- Specific, focused practice through a variety of exercises, including multiple-choice, short answer, and extended response questions

- A unique scaffolded layout that organizes questions in a way that challenges students to apply the standards in multiple formats

- "Fast Fact" boxes and a cumulative assessment in Mathematics and English Language Arts (ELA) to help students increase knowledge and demonstrate understanding across the standards

Perfect for in-school or at-home study, these engaging and versatile workbooks will help students meet and exceed the expectations of the Common Core.

Grade 2 Test Practice for Common Core
Maryrose Walsh and Judith Brendel
ISBN 978-1-4380-0550-8
Paperback, $14.99, *Can$16.99*

Grade 3 Test Practice for Common Core
Renee Snyder, M.A. and Susan M. Signet, M.A.
ISBN 978-1-4380-0551-5
Paperback, $14.99, *Can$16.99*

Grade 4 Test Practice for Common Core
Kelli Dolan and Shephali Chokshi-Fox
ISBN 978-1-4380-0515-7
Paperback, $14.99, *Can$16.99*

Grade 5 Test Practice for Common Core
Lisa M. Hall and Sheila Frye
ISBN 978-1-4380-0595-9
Paperback, $14.99, *Can$16.99*

Grade 6 Test Practice for Common Core
Christine R. Gray and Carrie Meyers-Herron
ISBN 978-1-4380-0592-8
Paperback, $14.99, *Can$16.99*

Barron's Educational Series, Inc.
250 Wireless Blvd.
Hauppauge, N.Y. 11788
Order toll-free: 1-800-645-3476

In Canada:
Georgetown Book Warehouse
34 Armstrong Ave.
Georgetown, Ontario L7G 4R9
Canadian orders: 1-800-247-7160

Prices subject to change without notice.

Coming soon to your local book store or visit **www.barronseduc.com**

(#295 R11/14)

Your Key to COMMON CORE SUCCESS

The recent implementation of Common Core Standards across the nation has offered new challenges to teachers, parents, and students. The **Common Core Success** series gives educators, parents, and children a clear-cut way to meet—and exceed—those grade-level goals.

Our English Language Arts (ELA) and Math workbooks are specifically designed to mirror the way teachers actually teach in the classroom. Each workbook is arranged to engage students and reinforce the standards in a meaningful way. This includes:

- Units divided into thematic lessons and designed for self-guided study
- "Stop and Think" sections throughout the ELA units, consisting of "Review," "Understand," and "Discover"
- "Ace It Time!" activities that offer a math-rich problem for each lesson

Students will find a wealth of practical information to help them master the Common Core!

Barron's Common Core Success
Grade K English Language Arts/Math
978-1-4380-0668-0

Barron's Common Core Success
Grade 1 English Language Arts
978-1-4380-0669-7

Barron's Common Core Success
Grade 1 Math
978-1-4380-0670-3

Barron's Common Core Success
Grade 2 English Language Arts
978-1-4380-0671-0

Barron's Common Core Success
Grade 2 Math
978-1-4380-0672-7

Barron's Common Core Success
Grade 3 English Language Arts
978-1-4380-0673-4

Barron's Common Core Success
Grade 3 Math
978-1-4380-0674-1

Barron's Common Core Success
Grade 4 English Language Arts
978-1-4380-0675-8

Barron's Common Core Success
Grade 4 Math
978-1-4380-0676-5

Barron's Common Core Success
Grade 5 English Language Arts
978-1-4380-0677-2

Barron's Common Core Success
Grade 5 Math
978-1-4380-0678-9

Barron's Common Core Success
Grade 6 English Language Arts
978-1-4380-0679-6

Barron's Common Core Success
Grade 6 Math
978-1-4380-0680-2

COMMON CORE SUCCESS WORKBOOKS GRADES K–6

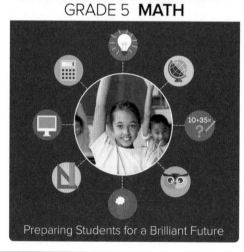

Each book:
Paperback,
8 3/8" x 10 7/8"
$12.99, Can$15.50

Available at your local book store
or visit **www.barronseduc.com**

Barron's Educational Series, Inc.
250 Wireless Blvd.
Hauppauge, N.Y. 11788
Order toll-free: 1-800-645-3476

Prices subject to change without notice.

In Canada:
Georgetown Book Warehouse
34 Armstrong Ave.
Georgetown, Ontario L7G 4R9
Canadian orders:
1-800-247-7160

(#293) R3/15